AMERICAN HEROES

★ ★ ★ 1735–1900 ★ ★ ★

By
MORRIE GREENBERG

Former English–Social Studies Consultant,
Los Angeles Unified School District

Brooke–Richards Press
Northridge, California

OTHER BOOKS BY MORRIE GREENBERG
The Buck Stops Here, A Biography of Harry Truman, Macmillan
We the People (multi-state history text adoptions, including California), D.C. Heath
Adventures in United States History
Survival in the Square, Brooke–Richards Press
American Adventures, Part 1, 1770–1870, Brooke–Richards Press
American Adventures, Part 2, 1870–Present, Brooke–Richards Press

Published by
Brooke-Richards Press
9420 Reseda Blvd., Suite 511
Northridge, California 91324

Copyright © 1998 by Morrie Greenberg

Printed in the United States of America

Library of Congress Cataloging-in-Publication Data
Greenberg, Morrie.
      American Heroes, 1735–1900 / Morrie Greenberg.
         p. cm.
      Summary: Fifteen true stories of American men and women all of whom became heroes through their work in different fields between 1735 and 1900.
      ISBN 0-9622652-3-3
         1. Heroes—United States—Biography—Juvenile literature.
2. United States—Biography—Juvenile literature. [1. Heroes.
2. United States—Biography.] I. Title
CT217.G68   1998
920.073—dc21
[b]

                                               98-22736
                                                CIP
                                                      AC

Contents

Acknowledgments

The author wishes to acknowledge the fine input provided by these teachers: George Rollins, Richard Tibbetts and Jon Borden.

Cover, book design and production, Jack Lanning. Editor, Audrey Bricker. Assistant editor, Brooke Sosa.

About the Author

Morrie Greenberg has served as a teacher, a department chairperson, an administrative consultant, and a school principal. As English-Social Studies consultant for the Los Angeles Unified School District, he worked with, and offered suggestions to, teachers at thirty different schools. He also taught Methods of Teaching Social Studies at California State University, Northridge, and coordinated a tutoring program for teenagers there. He is presently supervising student teachers at CSUN.

To the Reader

These are the men and women who **cared**, who thrived on challenges. No barrier could stop them. Inspired to make things better, they pushed on to pave the way for a better America. They are examples of America's many heroes.

WHY NOT make American history a story telling adventure? With that idea in mind, *American Adventures, Part One* and *Part Two* were published. *American Adventures'* overwhelming success led to another idea. Why not a series of story telling adventures that breathe the same life and meaning into America's past—and center on America's heroes? Here then, are the true stories of American men and women **who made a difference**, who helped make our country great. We think you will find their stories just as exciting and just as inspiring.

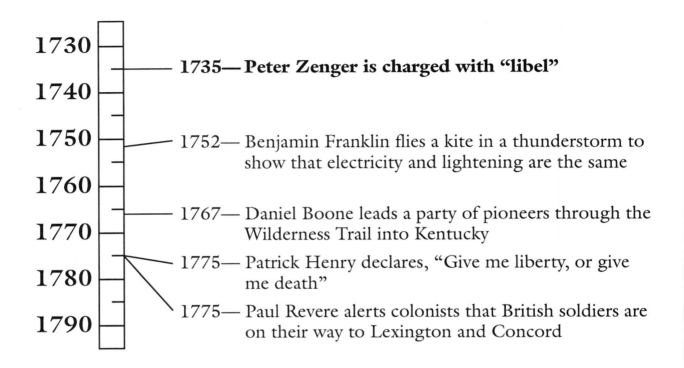

1730

1740 — 1735— **Peter Zenger is charged with "libel"**

1750 — 1752— Benjamin Franklin flies a kite in a thunderstorm to show that electricity and lightening are the same

1760

1770 — 1767— Daniel Boone leads a party of pioneers through the Wilderness Trail into Kentucky

1780 — 1775— Patrick Henry declares, "Give me liberty, or give me death"

1790 — 1775— Paul Revere alerts colonists that British soldiers are on their way to Lexington and Concord

A WORD ABOUT THE STORY

Peter Zenger
FREEDOM FIGHTER

He was a poor uneducated printer leading a simple life until the day two men entered his shop — and changed his life forever. Peter Zenger lived hundreds of years ago —even before the colonies became a nation — and yet, what he did is very important to all Americans living today.

The Verdict

"How can we make our governent better if people are not allowed to give opinions?"

PETER ZENGER looked at the judge first, then his eyes wandered across the crowded courtroom in search of his wife. When their eyes met, he nodded slightly. His wife smiled back. The year was 1735. For the past nine months Peter Zenger had spent his time in a tiny, wretched room they called a jail. There he sat staring at the four walls, or pacing back and forth perhaps a thousand times. When he had first arrived at the jail, the judge had given orders that "the prisoner will not be allowed pen, ink or paper." Only a crack in the jail's wooden door offered Peter a glimmer of hope. It was through this crack that he and his wife, Anna, whispered to one another on her regular visits.

For nine months Peter sat and stared, kept up his steady pacing, gulped down the awful tasting jail food, and tried his best to fight off the endless hours of boring loneliness. He had robbed no one, stolen nothing, hit no one. Nevertheless, he stood before a judge this August day in 1735, charged with a crime that could keep him in jail for months to come.

He gripped the railing in front of him firmly as the jury entered the courtroom.

"Have your reached a verdict?" the judge asked

"We have, your honor," one of the men on the jury answered.

Peter shot a nervous glance at his wife...

PETER ZENGER had left Germany bound for America with his mother and two younger brothers in 1710. Peter was only thirteen. Soon after the ship arrived in the New York colony, Peter found work as a printer's "apprentice," or helper. In these early colonial days, a boy did not go to a special school to learn a trade. Instead, he learned by working for a printer, a blacksmith, a carpenter, or some other craftsman. An apprentice was paid little or nothing for his work, but the "apprenticeship" gave a young person a chance to learn a craft. For the next eight years Peter worked as an apprentice. When Peter turned twenty-one, he was declared a "master" printer and went looking for work on his own. In time, he married and began his own business printing pamphlets and sermons.

One day two men came into Peter's small print shop. Peter stopped his work to greet them. The men told Peter that they wanted to start a newspaper and that they wanted him to print it. At this time there was only one newspaper in the whole New York colony.

"We will pay you for your work," they insisted.

"A newspaper?" Peter seemed genuinely surprised. "I would not know what to print." He started back towards his work. "I'm a printer, not a writer. I did not go to school in this country. I do not read or write well." While Peter had learned the printing trade, he was not an educated man.

One of the men smiled. "We want a news-paper that will speak out against the governor of New York."

"—but I would not know what to print," Peter repeated.

"We will do all the writing. You will only have to print what we give you." When Peter heard this, he said he would be willing to do the work.

Here the man paused, and looked straight at Peter. "But we have to tell you—if you do the printing, you might get in trouble."

The warning did not seem to bother Peter, and soon he was printing *The New York Weekly Gazette*, a small-sized four page newspaper. The paper came out each Monday, and Peter soon discovered why the man had told him that he might get into trouble. The King of England had selected, that is "appointed," a governor to rule the colony of New York. This governor was not popular with the colonists. Each week's paper carried a number of articles that attacked the governor. One article called him an idiot; another said that he acted like a tyrant or a dictator. The articles infuriated the royal governor. First, he ordered the papers burned in public; then he sent a soldier to Peter Zenger's home. The soldier threatened to hurt him if he did not stop printing the paper, but Peter refused to be frightened.

AT THIS TIME, it was against the law to print anything bad about the government or the men who ran the government—even if what you printed was true. The governor was anxious to have the men who wrote the articles arrested. However, the men were clever enough to print pseudonyms, that is, fake names, so that the governor was not sure who wrote the articles. The only one in the entire newspaper who used his correct name was Peter. There it was for all to see—PRINTER, PETER ZENGER.

The Governor gave the order to have Peter arrested and to charge him with libel, that is, with printing bad things about him.

Later that evening there was a knock at Peter's door. Peter was not surprised to find two policemen when he answered. He was under arrest, they informed him, for libel. A few days later Peter stood before a judge who set his bail for getting out of jail until his trial at 400 pounds. "Four hundred pounds?" Peter looked at the judge. "If I sell everything I own I will have but forty pounds."

"No matter," the judge answered. "If you can not put up your bail, you will stay in jail until the day of the trial." The governor wanted the judge to set the bail high, hoping that Peter Zenger would give out the names of the men who wrote the terrible things about him. Peter, however, refused to do this.

AND SO, Peter remained in jail. The days turned to weeks, the weeks to months. All the time, however, a strange thing was happening. Peter's wife continued to visit him regularly. He need not worry about the newspaper, she told him. She was seeing to it that his printing business and the newspaper continued. In all the time he was in jail, only one issue failed to come out. What is more, since his arrest, more people began reading the paper.

Nine months after he was placed in jail in 1735, Peter was brought to trial. The lawyers for the government reminded the jury that it was against the law to print anything bad about the government—whether what was printed was true or false.

When it was time for someone to speak for Peter, a gray-haired old man of eighty rose slowly from his chair. He was Andrew Hamilton, a highly respected lawyer from Philadelphia. He had volunteered to help Peter without pay. The men on the jury leaned forward, eager to hear what he had to say. "People should not be afraid to criticize, or speak out against the government," Hamilton said. "How can we make our government better, how can we correct wrongs if people are not allowed to give opinions freely? How can we have a good government, how can we be free, if someone is afraid of being jailed for what is printed in a newspaper?"

The jury was dismissed to talk over, that is, to deliberate, a decision. Ten minutes later, the jury was back in the courtroom.

"Have you reached a verdict?" the judge inquired.

"Yes, we have, Your Honor. We find the defendant not guilty."

The citizens in the courtroom cheered their approval of the verdict. The judge pounded his gavel. "Order! Order!" he shouted, but there would be no order that day. The citizens were too excited over the verdict not to shout. Peter Zenger was willing to stay in jail for nine months, willing to endure the pain of loneliness, willing not to tell on his friends, all for an idea. The idea of freedom of the press. The idea that a man or woman could print or speak out against the government without fear of being charged with a crime, or prosecuted.

SOME 56 YEARS after Peter Zenger's trial, in 1791, the wise men who sat down to write the Bill of Rights for the United States Constitution reminded one another of the Peter Zenger trial. They wanted to make certain that Americans would have the freedom to say and print whatever they wanted. And so they wrote the First Amendment to the U.S. Constitution guaranteeing to all Americans freedom of speech and freedom of the press. The trial of Peter Zenger would never be forgotten.

Writing Activities

1. GETTING OUT THE WORD

Find the word or words closest to the meaning of the underlined word in each sentence. Then, copy the sentence, using the word or words in place of the underlined word.

1. He spent his time in a <u>wretched</u> jail.

    very old   horrible   dirty   very dusty

2. The King of England <u>appointed</u> the governor.

    selected   warned   fired   scolded

3. He worked as an <u>apprentice</u> for a printer.

    beginner   laborer   reader   janitor

4. One article said the governor was a <u>tyrant</u>.

    swindler   mad person   dictator   thief

5. The governor was <u>infuriated</u> by what he read.

    outraged   pleased   annoyed   bothered

6. The writers used <u>pseudonyms</u>.

    fake headlines   fake names   fake stories   fake addresses

7. The newspaper <u>criticized</u> the government.

    praised   warned   ignored   found fault with

8. Peter Zenger was <u>prosecuted</u> for what was in the newspaper.

    picked on   found guilty   found not guilty   charged with a crime

2. WHAT'S THE MESSAGE?

Copy out the ONE sentence that you think is the story's most important message or idea.

A. Knowing how to argue in a court is very important.

B. Keeping someone in jail a long time is cruel.

C. Freedom of the press and freedom of speech are very important.

D. Speaking out against your government is wrong.

Let's Talk—Discussion Activities

3. THINK IT THROUGH

Do you think you should be arrested if you—

— say the mayor of the city is a poor mayor.

— write a newspaper article saying the mayor is too lazy to do a good job.

— hold up a sign that says the mayor is dumb.

— hit the mayor on his head with a sign that says he is dumb.

4. TODAY

Today, a person charged with a crime can usually put up a certain amount of money—called bail—to guarantee that he will show up in court. By doing this the person does not have to stay in the jail until the day of the trial. Take one side or the other:

— Letting someone out of jail on bail is a good idea.

— Letting someone out of jail on bail is a poor idea.

You hear someone say: "People should not be allowed to speak out against the government." How would you answer this person?

5. WHERE'S THE HERO?

What made Peter Zenger a hero? Pick out what YOU consider the THREE best answers.

— He did not like to be in jail.

— He was loyal to his friends.

— He was willing to suffer for what he believed in.

— He was a good printer.

— He fought for what he thought was right.

— He did not like the governor.

Cooperative Group or Research Activities

6. LOOK IT UP

Select one of the persons listed on the time line for this story. Use other books or articles to gather more information about the person, and then make a presentation explaining why the person might be considered a hero.

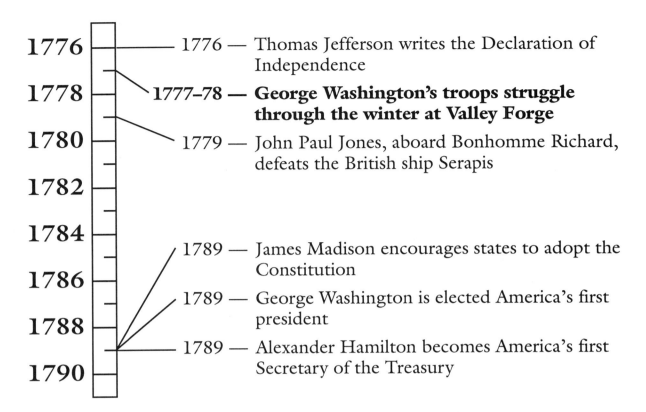

1776

1778

1780

1782

1784

1786

1788

1790

1776 — Thomas Jefferson writes the Declaration of Independence

1777–78 — George Washington's troops struggle through the winter at Valley Forge

1779 — John Paul Jones, aboard Bonhomme Richard, defeats the British ship Serapis

1789 — James Madison encourages states to adopt the Constitution

1789 — George Washington is elected America's first president

1789 — Alexander Hamilton becomes America's first Secretary of the Treasury

A WORD ABOUT THE STORY

George Washington
GENERAL/PRESIDENT/STATESMAN

Many years ago someone wrote that George Washington was, "First in war, first in peace and first in the hearts of his countrymen." HERO AT VALLEY FORGE helps us understand just what the writer meant. Today, many of our cities, mountains, rivers, and even a state, are named after our first president. And, of course, our nation's capital honors the name Washington.

Hero at Valley Forge

A TIRED General George Washington pushed back the canvas flap and entered his tent. Inside, there was little protection from the cold night air. Washington rubbed his hands together deep in his own thoughts. He had marched his troops this late December day in 1777 to Valley Forge, just outside of Philadelphia. Here, he decided, the soldiers of the Continental Army would camp. They would stay at Valley Forge and wait for the first signs of spring. In spring, they would stir themselves and resume fighting the British. And so, the soldiers of the Continental Army set up their tents, then prayed for decent weather.

It was not to be.

December brought blustering snowstorms that swept across the land day after day. The soldiers' lives became living nightmares. They trudged through snow in shoes worn through the soles—or with no shoes at all. Their tattered uniforms offered little resistance to the chilling wind, and the bonfires they built to warm themselves set up gloomy, swirling smoke patterns that choked them when the wind shifted. At dinnertime, the soldiers often had to spit out their food—it was not fit to eat. Washington wondered: How long could they go on like this—thousands of soldiers without proper food, with clothing in shreds, and many without shoes?

Washington's face was drawn and stern as he took a seat at his desk in the tent. He grasped a quill pen. Images of what he had seen that day were still fresh in his mind. The soldiers suffered so—yet few of them complained. Meantime, the lawmakers in Pennsylvania were whining to him in letters and in the newspapers. Why, they demanded to know, had his army stopped fighting? Why had he taken his soldiers into winter quarters instead of attacking the British soldiers?

W ASHINGTON sat a moment deep in thought, then dipped his quill in the ink. "I can assure those gentleman," he scrawled, "that it is a much easier and less distressing to complain in a comfortable room by a good fireside than to occupy a cold bleak hill and sleep under frost and snow with little clothing. Though these gentlemen seem to have little feeling for the poor soldiers, I have great pity for them." He reminded the colonial lawmakers that he had seen "men without blankets to lay on, men without shoes—so that their marches could be traced by the blood from their feet—and, almost as often, without food as with, marching through frost and snow, and at Christmas taking up their winter quarters within a day's march of the enemy, without a house or hut to cover them."

As far as Washington was concerned, no army in history had stood up to hardships with more bravery.

George Washington had never wanted to take charge of the Continental Army. When he was young, he helped the British army against the French during the French and Indian War. He was an excellent soldier who knew how to fight in America's wilderness. But he had gladly given up being a soldier and returned to his plantation in Mt. Vernon, Virginia. He remained at Mt. Vernon for the next fifteen years. Then, in the early 1770's, the British began to tax the colonies without the colonists' permission. Washington joined the other patriots who protested, "No taxation without representation."

In 1775 a group of protesting colonists representing twelve of the thirteen colonies met at Philadelphia. Though fighting had already broken out against the British at Lexington and Concord, most of the colonists did not want to break away from England. They wanted England to stop these unfair taxes and to let them rule themselves. However, they did want to be ready with an army if the British did not pay any attention to their pleas. The army would be called the "Continental Army."

The Continental army was not a real army from a real "nation." Its soldiers were men from the different colonies who were willing to serve as soldiers, but only for short periods of time. It was not a well trained army, and it would have to face one of the best armies in the world supplied by the best navy in the world.

GEORGE WASHINGTON was chosen to lead this army. He hated the thought of going to war. However, he put aside his own personal wishes. He felt a deep sense of duty to all the colonies. He hoped that the British would "come to their senses," but the British made no attempt to stop the harsh laws. The fighting continued and on July 4, 1776, the thirteen colonies declared themselves free from England. Washington still lead the army, but now the colonies were fighting for independence.

The war had been going on for almost two years when Washington took his place at Valley Forge, and it would drag on another three. The colonists had some help from the French navy, but it was the courage and the spirit of the Continental army led by George Washington that gave the colonies their victory. The peace treaty with England was signed in 1783. The colonies were free states now! However, things did not go well for the thirteen states. They quarreled with one another; they had trouble trading with other countries; they often had no money to pay their bills. There was a central or main government, but it was very weak.

ABOUT THIS TIME a respected army colonel wrote a letter to George Washington who had gone back to his plantation at Mt. Vernon in Virginia. He reminded Washington how bad things were. Then he got to the point: "We need the kind of leadership that led us to victory in the War for Independence. We need a king." It was clear what he was saying: We want to start an American monarchy and make you, George Washington, our first king. Many other people also favored making Washington king.

Most of the countries of Europe at this time had kings and queens. Tall and handsome, with keen blue-gray eyes, Washington certainly would have made a fine looking king. He was, in fact, the most respected man in all the thirteen states. Without him, the colonist would have lost the war. There was little

"The soldiers suffered so..."

question that Washington could be king if he wanted to, but Washington wasted no time in writing an answer to the colonel.

"Sir, with a mixture of great surprise and astonishment, I have read your letter," he wrote, "Nothing in the course of the war has given me more pain. You could not have found a person to whom your ideas are more disagreeable. If you have any regard for your country, stop these thoughts and never say them again."

In 1789 a new Constitution created a republic—not a monarchy—with a stronger central government. The country would have an elected president, not a king or a queen.

The first U.S. president to be elected was, of course, George Washington. As a general and then as President, Washington gave much to his country, but his greatest gift may well have been the loud "No!" he gave when some people wanted to make him king. As the first president, George Washington set many excellent examples on the best way to rule in a republic. Other presidents followed his examples.

Washington never became a king, but in later years he came to be called, "The father of his country." He certainly would have liked that title better.

Writing Activities

1. GETTING OUT THE WORD

Find the word or words closest to the meaning of the underlined word in each sentence. Then, copy the sentence, using the word or words in place of the underlined word.

1. The army <u>resumed</u> fighting in the spring.
   again started   stopped   started   slowed down

2. The soldiers marched through the <u>blustering</u> snow storms.
   freezing   very windy   white   slightly breezy

3. They <u>trudged</u> through the snow.
   ran   fell   tramped   wandered

4. Their uniforms were <u>tattered</u>.
   old   dirty   bloodied   torn to shreds

5. George Washington wrote with a <u>quill</u> pen.
   metal   leather   wooden   feather

6. The colonists <u>protested</u> the taxes.
   complained about   worried about   wrote about   paid

7. The British refused to change the <u>harsh</u> laws.
   new   cruel   unfair   old

8. Some Americans wanted to start a country ruled by a <u>monarch</u>.
   president   king or queen   Congress   wise ruler

2. WHAT'S THE MESSAGE?

Copy out the ONE sentence that you think is the story's most important message or idea.

A. Washington and his soldiers suffered a great deal to win our freedom from Great Britain.

B. The British king did not understand the American colonists.

C. Americans owe a great deal to all their generals.

D. Bad weather can keep an army from fighting.

Let's Talk—Discussion Activities

3. THINK IT THROUGH

Why is it more important for a person to be educated in a republic than in a country ruled by a king or queen?

Why was it so important for the first U.S. President to do things right? Isn't one president as important as another? Explain your answer.

4. TODAY

George Washington is remembered in many different ways. Name five or more places named after our first president (look at a map).

Imagine that a time machine brings George Washington back to modern day America. What three questions would you like to ask him.

5. WHERE'S THE HERO?

What made George Washington a hero? Pick out what YOU consider the three BEST answers.

He was tall and handsome.

He cared about the soldiers he commanded.

He refused to make himself a king.

He was willing to make great sacrifices.

He was a good surveyor and a good horseman.

Cooperative Group or Research Activities

6. LOOK IT UP

Select one of the persons listed on the time line for this story. Use other books or articles to gather more information about the person, and then make a presentation explaining why the person might be considered a hero.

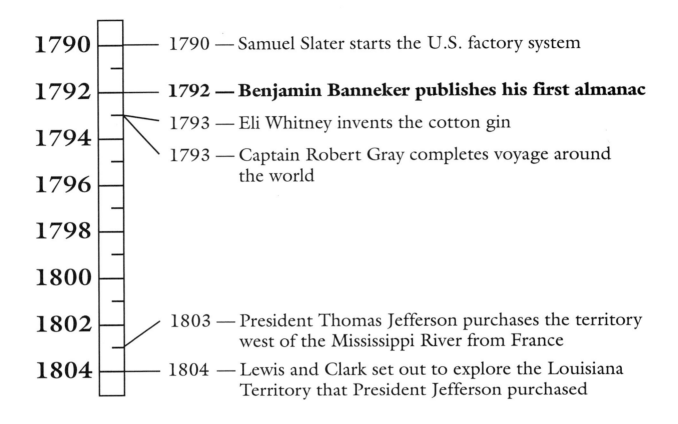

1790 — Samuel Slater starts the U.S. factory system

1792 — Benjamin Banneker publishes his first almanac

1793 — Eli Whitney invents the cotton gin

1793 — Captain Robert Gray completes voyage around the world

1803 — President Thomas Jefferson purchases the territory west of the Mississippi River from France

1804 — Lewis and Clark set out to explore the Louisiana Territory that President Jefferson purchased

A WORD ABOUT THE STORY

Benjamin Banneker
ASTRONOMER

There was no reason to believe that Benjamin Banneker would be anyone special. His father, once a slave, made his living farming. Young Benjamin, like almost all of his Maryland neighbors, would surely grow up to farm for the rest of his life. Or would he? What "door" would open to change his life forever?

The Amazing Banneker

A STRANGER WALKING by this one farm just outside of Baltimore, Maryland, in 1786 would have been flabbergasted! There were farmers on either side plowing the rich soil, sowing seeds, cultivating the land, or harvesting different crops. On the other hand, here was this one farm covered with weeds and looking so deserted. If the stranger stopped to ask one of the hard working neighbors about the forsaken looking farm, one of the neighbors might stop working long enough to say, "Oh, that's Benjamin Banneker's farm. Benjamin is there all right, but he's more likely than not fast asleep in his cabin right now."

The stranger was sure to be surprised. "Asleep? In the middle of the day—when there's so much farm work to be done! Sounds like a pretty strange fellow to me."

"Strange?" the neighbor might say. "You think that is strange? Let me tell you what Benjamin Banneker did. See that cabin of his—take a close look." The stranger looked. "Why," he exclaimed, "He's gone and put a window in his roof! Now who ever heard of a window in a roof?"

"Oh, but that's not all," the neighbor adds. "If you come around here late at night—you'll see him lying on the dirt over there just looking up at the sky. Yes, you heard me right—and he lies there for hours at a time."

At this point, the stranger might walk away shaking his head at the strange habits of this Maryland farmer.

THE TRUTH OF THE MATTER was that Benjamin Banneker was not strange at all. In fact, he was pretty intelligent. Benjamin was born near Baltimore in the colony of Maryland in 1731. His ancestors had been brought to America from Africa as slaves. After years of hard work, Benjamin's father saved enough to buy his freedom. As a free man, he purchased 100 acres of land and set about raising tobacco and other crops on his own. When Benjamin was born, because his father was no longer a slave, Benjamin was free as well. When he was four years old, Benjamin's grandmother read the Bible to him. He listened so intently she decided to use the Bible to teach him how to read. There were few if any schools for black children in the 1700s, but there was a school near his home for both black and white children. He went there for a short time. He loved to read and write and—best of all—to do arithmetic.

Numbers fascinated Benjamin, and, as he grew older, he never lost his interest in numbers. He learned many other things on his own. He loved to look up at the sky and stare at the clouds and watch the weather change. He learned to play the violin and the flute, and he read whenever he could. However, like most young men who lived in the 1700s, Benjamin spent most of his time working on the family farm. When his parents died, he took over running the farm, but his heart was never in farming. Young Banneker had a yearning to do more.

When Benjamin was still in his twenties, he decided that he wanted to build a clock. Very few people owned clocks in these days. As a matter of fact, Benjamin had never even seen the inside of a clock! Anyone could have told Benjamin: "How can you build a clock? You don't have the tools or the training or the experience. And you don't even have the metal it takes to build one." No matter. There was a peddler who came around the area, and he had a pocket watch. Benjamin borrowed it and looked inside. He saw how the wheels turned, how the gears meshed with one another, where the minute and hour hands were placed, how the spring wound and unwound. Then, Benjamin simply announced that he would build a clock.

INSTEAD OF METAL WHEELS, Benjamin used flat, circular pieces of wood. Instead of special tools, he used a knife and whittled "teeth" around each piece of wood so that each piece became a wheel that fit or meshed with the other. By now, Benjamin knew his mathematics well. He figured out the exact size each wheel had to be so that it turned exactly right. A clock was very rare in these days, and so when Banneker announced that his clock was finished, many people who lived around Baltimore came to see and

admire it—and to check whether or not it was accurate. There was no need to worry. Banneker had build the clock carefully. It kept the right time for forty years!

As the years went by, Benjamin read as much as he could and stayed interested in many things. Work on his farm still took up most of his day— until something happened that changed his life forever...

BENJAMIN BORROWED some books on astronomy—the study of the stars, the sun, the moon, and the planets—as well as a telescope. He was fascinated by what he saw and read, and when Benjamin discovered all the mathematical calculations that were a part of astronomy he grew even more excited. Soon he was spending his nights with his eyes cast in the heavens, making calculations and sketching and writing down his observations. The next day, when it was time to work, Banneker was too exhausted to do his farm chores. When winter came, and it was too cold to spend long hours outside, Benjamin got an idea: Why not cut a hole in the roof and make a window so that he could watch the skies from his warm cabin?

In 1790 Congress passed a bill to set up a capital city on the Potomac River for the new nation. Many states wanted the capital to be in their state. However, the founding fathers thought it would be best to have a capital that would not be a part of any state. That way it would be the capital for the whole country. Virginia and Maryland agreed to give up some of their land for what was then called the "Federal Territory," and would later be called "Washington, D.C." In order to plot or know exactly where the Federal Territory was, it would have to be surveyed with special instruments by a group of "surveyors" who would then place this information on maps. They would also survey where each government building would be located. By this time, the skill of Benjamin Banneker as a mathematician was well known around Maryland. He was asked to come and help survey the new capital. He gladly accepted and did a good job as part of the survey team. By late April of 1791, however, Banneker decided it was time to return to his cabin. He had left some important "unfinished" business there.

FOR YEARS, BENJAMIN had been writing down all the information he could about the sun, moon, stars, and the planets. In these early days, farmers depended on books called almanacs. An almanac would tell a farmer what time the sun would rise and set for every day of the year. It gave the phases of the moon and when the tide was high and low. It told when fall, winter, spring, summer began and ended. By looking at an almanac a farmer could tell the best time of year to plant crops, what kind of weather to expect, the nights there would be a quarter, half, and full moons—along with other information. Banneker decided that he would make an almanac of his own. He believed his almanac would be a big help to farmers everywhere.

And so, he went on studying the sky at night, reading more astronomy books, taking notes, making mathematical calculations. This left him no time to take care of his farm. While he was working on the survey, his sister took care of his farm. Now she was back in her own home. Banneker had a choice: he could take care of his farm or finish his almanac.

For years Banneker had been writing down all the information he could. (Pictured: cover of one of Banneker's Almanacs)

When Banneker's first almanac came out in 1792, he knew he had made the right decision. Farmers in the Southern states began using his almanac, and he kept publishing new ones for the next five years. Yes, he had neglected the work on his own farm, but, he was helping many other farmers. Benjamin Banneker had good reason to feel proud.

Writing Activities

1. GETTING OUT THE WORD

Find the word or words closest to the meaning of the underlined word in each sentence. Then, copy the sentence, using the word or words in place of the underlined word.

1. The visitor was <u>flabbergasted</u> when he saw the farm.
   astonished   unhappy   discouraged   disappointed

2. The farmers were <u>sowing</u> seeds.
   harvesting   watering   gathering up   planting

3. Banneker had <u>a yearning</u> to do other things.
   a reminder   a strong desire   the experience   the training

4. He saw how the gears <u>meshed</u>.
   fitted together   disconnected   detached   separated

5. Banneker's <u>ancestors</u> came from Africa.
   parents   children   relatives who lived before him   grandfathers

6. Banneker was good at <u>making calculations</u>.
   using numbers   studying the stars   astronomy   sketching

7. Banneker wrote and published an <u>almanac</u>.
   a book for factory workers   a book for surveyors
   a book for farmers   a book for visitors to America

8. He <u>neglected</u> his own farm.
   ignored   stopped watering   rented   gave away

2. WHAT'S THE MESSAGE?

Copy out the ONE sentence what you think is the story's most important message or idea.

A. Educate yourself so that you can reach your goal.

B. Farming is hard work.

C. Be willing to admire someone even if he acts silly.

D. Almanacs give farmers important information.

Let's Talk—Discussion Activities

3. THINK IT THROUGH

Some people seem to have a "hunger for learning." What do you think this means?

Do you think Benjamin Banneker's father was a hero in some way? Explain your answer.

4. TODAY

How do today's farmers find out about weather conditions?

5. WHERE'S THE HERO?

What made Benjamin Banneker a hero? Pick out what YOU consider the THREE best answers.

He stuck to his goals.

He taught himself.

He was a good astronomer.

He was once a good farmer.

His accomplishments helped other people.

Cooperative Group or Research Activities

6. LOOK IT UP

Select one of the persons listed on the time line for this story. Use other books or articles to gather more information about the person, and then make a presentation explaining why the person might be considered a hero.

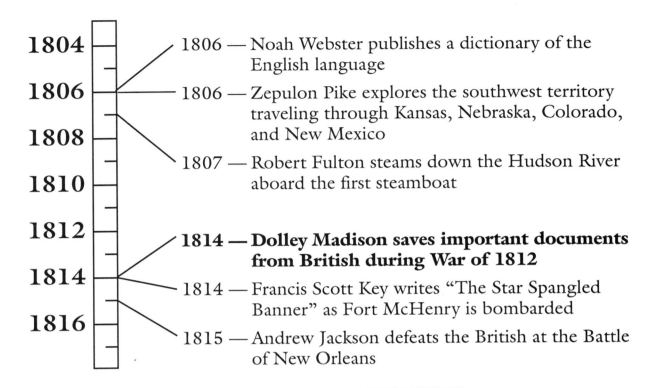

1804

1806

1808

1810

1812

1814

1816

1806 — Noah Webster publishes a dictionary of the English language

1806 — Zepulon Pike explores the southwest territory traveling through Kansas, Nebraska, Colorado, and New Mexico

1807 — Robert Fulton steams down the Hudson River aboard the first steamboat

1814 — Dolley Madison saves important documents from British during War of 1812

1814 — Francis Scott Key writes "The Star Spangled Banner" as Fort McHenry is bombarded

1815 — Andrew Jackson defeats the British at the Battle of New Orleans

A WORD ABOUT THE STORY

Reproduced from the Collections of the LIBRARY OF CONGRESS

Dolley Madison

Dolley Madison
FIRST LADY

First she captured the heart of James Madison, then the heart of the young nation. But what was so special about Dolley Madison? After all, it was her husband who helped write the Constitution and later became the president of the United States. What did Dolley ever do?

A Nation's First Lady

DOLLEY'S HEART seemed to skip a beat. *Were those the sounds of hoofbeats?* She listened as they grew louder and louder—then stopped. An anxious Dolley dropped the papers she was holding and raced towards the front of the house. She flung the heavy front door open in time to see an American army officer dismount from his horse and walk towards her.

"I have a message," he called, "—from your husband." He paused a moment to catch his breath. "There is danger if you do not leave at once." He did not have to say more. She could hear the rumble of the distant cannons. The soldiers in red uniforms were marching towards the capital! She would do what her husband said. After all, he was the President of the United States!

JAMES MADISON was sworn in as the fourth president of the United States on March 4, 1809. About this time, British seamen were boarding American ships and taking away some of the Americans on board. The British claimed that the sailors they took were once British subjects and were needed to fight for England in their war against France. Madison felt he could not let the British get away with this. On June 18, 1812, the United States Congress declared war on Great Britain.

At first, the British were too busy fighting the French in Europe, but on an August morning in 1814, a huge fleet of British ships landed in Chesapeake Bay, near Washington. Thousands upon thousands of British troops disembarked. *Where would they march?* Some Americans thought they would move on to Baltimore, Maryland, but others feared they would strike the nation's capital—at this time called "Washington City."

President James Madison and his wife, Dolley were in the presidential mansion in Washington City when news reached them that the large British army was probably moving towards Washington. Madison began packing important government documents into large wooden crates. He would leave immediately to join American troops camped nearby. Citizens were already leaving the city. He urged Dolley to do the same, but she insisted on staying. Madison only looked at her.

"All right," he cautioned. "But be ready to leave at once with these crates if the British move towards Washington."

Dolley stayed at the mansion packing more of the "state papers" and listening to the creaking sounds of horse-drawn wagons outside. When she glanced out her windows she could see people moving out of the city in carriages and wagons stacked high with belongings. "I'm not going to leave," Dolley thought to herself. And then the message came—*the Redcoats were marching straight toward the capital!* England was about to give the new nation a lesson it would not soon forget.

CORBIS-BETTMANN

Dolley stayed at the mansion packing important state papers. (Pictured: An early artist's idea of the event.)

DOLLEY THANKED the officer who brought her the news, then rushed outside long enough to convince two strong looking citizens to come inside and help her. The officer and the two men placed the crates filled with the important government papers on board a wagon. Then, as she moved towards the front door, Dolley glanced at the huge framed painting of George Washington mounted on the wall. "We can't leave that for the British," she cried. The men started to unscrew the large frame from the wall. *This was taking too long!*

"Get an ax," Dolley ordered. "We will simply smash the frame and take the canvas."

Before long, a heavily laden horse drawn wagon and a carriage carrying Dolley were rolling away from the President's mansion, away from the advancing British army. As the wagon bumped slowly along the road that would take them to the countryside, Dolley had time to think—this was not the first time she had fled from a city...

WHEN DOLLEY was a young lady in her twenties she lived in Philadelphia, and was married to a lawyer named John Todd. They had two boys—a four year old and an infant less than a year old. One day her husband came home ashen faced. "The fever has struck our city." He did not have to say more. The "fever" was yellow fever, a terrible illness. Before long, thousands and thousands of citizens were running away from Philadelphia. The year was 1793. Philadelphia was the nation's capital and its largest city. Dolley's husband insisted that Dolley leave the city with their two children. He would follow later, he told her. He would stay only long enough to care for his parents who had already been struck by the disease.

And so Dolley fled from Philadelphia to live with relatives in a small town—fleeing, she thought, from the terrible plague. It was not to be. She caught "the fever." She knew that the illness was killing thousands of people! She wondered if she would survive as she drifted into a deep sleep. Days later a groggy Dolley awakened only to learn that the wretched disease had killed her husband and her infant child. This was a terrible blow, but Dolley would not let the tragedy destroy her life. Much later, Dolley and James Madison fell in love with one another and were married.

AS DOLLEY'S CARRIAGE bumped along the country road away from Washington, Dolley must have realized that once again she was a "survivor." She had done her duty. The papers were safe. And so was the portrait of George Washington. She would never let this symbol fall into British hands. But what about the presidential mansion?

By now, Dolley was miles away from Washington. She had no way of knowing that British troops were moving from one government building to another. Inside each building they stacked furniture and whatever wood they could find, then set the wood afire with blazing torches. One building after another went up in flames. When night fell, Dolley and the others who had fled the capital could see the glare of the flames that licked the night sky. Dolley could only wonder about the fate of the president's home.

The next day a terrible storm struck the Washington area. No one could remember a storm with such a fury. Gales ripped the roofs off of houses; streets were soon strewn with fallen trees. Anyone trying to walk was bowled over, and a torrent of steady rain pounded and flooded the ground. After a number of soldiers had been battered and killed by the storm, the British decided to leave Washington.

WHEN THE STORM finally cleared, an anxious Dolley, together with President Madison, journeyed back to Washington. Her heart sank as she approached what had once been home. The Presidential mansion was a scorched skeleton with walls. *What a sad sight!* Some citizens thought that the Americans should give up and stop the war. Madison would not hear of such a thing. In time the war ended and the British agreed to stop bothering American ships. It was a time for the nation to rejoice. The presidential home would be rebuilt—and renamed "The White House." (James and Dolley Madison would never live there, however. By the time it was completed, Madison was no longer president.)

There had only been two first ladies before Dolley—Martha Washington and Abigail Adams. The third President, Thomas Jefferson's wife had died and he was a widower. The two First Ladies had chosen to politely "stay in the background." Dolley could not do this. She was a dynamic, outgoing person who always seemed interested in others. "I don't care what office a person has," she once said. "I care only about people." She brought a "style" to the capital with her warmth and independence. The people loved her for it. When Madison won the presidency, his opponent said, "I did not lose to Madison. I lost to Mr. and Mrs. Madison.

DOLLEY SET A TONE, a way of doing things, that First ladies could follow for the next two centuries. She never thought of herself as a hero, but her graciousness, her love of people, and her warm regard for others of all backgrounds left a mark that would last for the next two centuries.

And—always so it seemed—Americans liked to recall how she saved the symbol of our country's beginning, the Washington portrait. Though this was Dolley's "claim to fame," there was much more to Dolley. Dolley Madison lived a long life. She stayed close to every American President from our first, George Washington, to our twelfth president, Zachary Taylor. When she died in 1845, President Taylor declared, "What a great lady. She will never be forgotten because she was truly our first lady for a half century." Dolley, like the portrait of George Washington, remains a symbol of America's past, America's way of life.

Writing Activities

1. GETTING OUT THE WORD

Find the word or words closest to the meaning of the underlined word in each sentence. Then, copy the sentence, using the word or words in place of the underlined word.

1. When the horse arrived, the officer <u>dismounted</u>.
   left   saluted   got on   got off

2. The British kept <u>boarding</u> American ships.
   shooting at   going on   ramming   stopping.

3. Thousands of troops <u>disembarked</u> from the ship
   rioted   ran away   boarded the ship   left

4. He looked <u>ashen</u> faced.
   tired   ill   thin   pale

5. She took the <u>portrait</u> with her.
   large painting   old painting   painting of a person
   painting of a famous person

6. She was <u>groggy</u> when she woke up.
   sleepy   crying   hungry   upset

7. She thought it was important to save this <u>symbol</u>.
   old portrait   thing that stands for something
   important painting   document

8. Dolley was a <u>dynamic</u> person.
   honest   energetic   friendly   caring

2. WHAT'S THE MESSAGE?

Copy out the ONE sentence that you think is the story's most important message or idea.

A. Yellow fever was a dangerous disease.

B. The United States Won the war of 1812.

C. Dolley Madison set a good example for future First Ladies.

D. The White House symbolizes freedom.

Let's Talk—Discussion Activities

3. THINK IT THROUGH

Take one side or the other:

A First Lady should stay in the background—she is not the one who was elected.

A First Lady represents our country too. She should get involved in things to help the country.

4. TODAY

How should we expect a "First Man" to act when a woman is elected president? What should we expect him to do?

5. WHERE'S THE HERO?

What made Dolley Madison a hero? Pick out what YOU consider the THREE best answers.

She was married to President James Madison.

She was brave in difficult times.

She cared about other people.

She lived through a terrible epidemic.

She set a good example for other First Ladies.

Cooperative Group or Research Activities

6. LOOK IT UP

Select one of the persons listed on the time line for this story. Use other books or articles to gather more information about the person, and then make a presentation explaining why the person might be considered a hero.

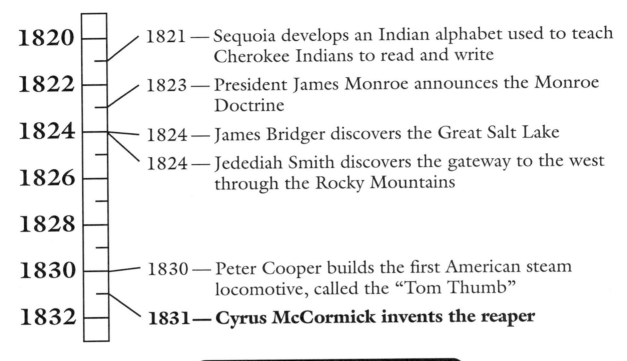

1820

1822

1824

1826

1828

1830

1832

1821 — Sequoia develops an Indian alphabet used to teach Cherokee Indians to read and write

1823 — President James Monroe announces the Monroe Doctrine

1824 — James Bridger discovers the Great Salt Lake

1824 — Jedediah Smith discovers the gateway to the west through the Rocky Mountains

1830 — Peter Cooper builds the first American steam locomotive, called the "Tom Thumb"

1831 — Cyrus McCormick invents the reaper

A WORD ABOUT THE STORY

Cyrus McCormick
INVENTOR

Not many people can claim they changed the world. Cyrus McCormick certainly did not start out with that in mind. He just had an idea his father gave him—an idea to make things better and easier for farmers. There was just one problem: the idea did not work.

Cyrus McCormick

The Farmer Who Changed the World

IF SOMEONE ASKED YOU to name the world's greatest inventions, what inventions would you choose? The airplane? the automobile? television? the computer? Any chance at all that you would pick an invention that—but wait. Let's not get ahead of our story...

CYRUS STARED AT HIS FATHER hunched over the contraption of wheels, gears, belts, and wires. Beads of sweat poured down his father's wrinkled face, and his bare arms showed fresh cuts and bruises.

"I can't see how to get this thing workin' right," he said. "First I try it one way, then I try it another way. No matter what I do, it just won't cut the wheat right, Cyrus." His father stood up now, his eyes squinting to block out the late afternoon sun. His callused hands brushed at the dirt and mud left on his clothes from crawling under the machine. "Well, let's go get washed up, son. It'll still be here tomorrow."

Cyrus picked up his rake and hoe. The two men made long shadows across the farm as they trudged towards the farmhouse. Cyrus felt his muscles ache with each step. It would be good to get back to the house where he could wash and rest. Farming in western Virginia in 1830 was hard work even for a husky twenty-one year old like Cyrus.

When they reached the farmhouse door, the old man broke the silence. "Maybe it's time I give up," he said. "Maybe it's time to let someone else, someone a little fresher, figure out a way to cut the wheat so that it doesn't end up all crushed." They went inside. "—and with a machine that doesn't keep breakin' down so much."

Cyrus had heard his father talk this way before, but he always managed to drift back to the machine a week or two later. This time, however, Cyrus caught something in his father's expression—in his eyes and in his voice—that told Cyrus that his father meant it. *Twenty years of trying was long enough.*

That night, tired as he was, Cyrus had trouble falling asleep. He pictured his father's invention in his mind. He watched the big wheel move along the ground and the gears mesh in place. He saw the cutter slashing the wheat as a horse pulled the machine across a large field. Maybe, he thought, if the big wheel were moved closer to the cutter, and the belt—.

The next day, Cyrus did not stop thinking about the machine. Before long, he was spending every spare minute outside of his farm duties working on the machine. After a bit of tinkering Cyrus realized he would have to think of a design quite different from what his father had tried. He worked on the new design for months. By the summer of 1831, Cyrus felt ready to test his invention.

A neighbor had agreed to let Cyrus use his large wheat field for the test. One early summer morning some thirty neighbors gathered to watch the experiment. A slight breeze rustled the wheat—it was certainly ready for harvesting.

Young Cyrus McCormick surveyed the crowd. Though quite nervous, he offered them a warm smile. A grizzled farmer friend called out from the knot of onlookers. "Hope you have better luck than your pa." Cyrus walked over to pat the gray horse harnessed to the machine, then took his place on a rickety seat to the right and in front of a large wheel that looked like a paddle wheel on a ship. If all went well, the wheel would press the grain against some iron fingers that separated the stalks of wheat. Then knives would work back and forth cutting the wheat, and the harvested wheat would land on a wooden platform.

Cyrus gripped the reins firmly, and took a deep breath. "Giddyup," he shouted.

The horse—harnessed off to the side to keep it from trampling the wheat—strained forward, and the large wheel creaked into motion. The crowed stood silent now. *Would that contraption really cut the wheat?*

CYRUS STEERED THE HORSE in a straight line. In minutes, a narrow strip of land marked where the wheat had disappeared! People in the crowd began to point and murmur. The wheat began piling up on the platform behind Cyrus. A man and a woman walking alongside the contraption

raked the wheat from the platform as fast as they could. Now the machine turned and began to mow down another row. By now the onlookers were yelling and shouting and congratulating each other.

When Cyrus finally pulled on the reigns and brought the horse to a halt, the small crowd surged towards him, but it was his father who got to him first. "It works! It works!" his father said over and over. And it did "work," but Cyrus soon discovered his problems with the wheat cutting machine were far from over.

CYRUS McCORMICK started manufacturing his machines, called "reapers," and selling them to the farmers in the South. His earliest reapers, however, were no match for the rolling hills and stubborn rocks in this part of the country. A horse pulling the contraption up a hill would tire quickly, and the machines broke down too often. McCormick kept working, hoping somehow to overcome these problems. Then, one day he told a friend that he had decided to take a trip to the Midwest. When the friend asked him why, McCormick only smiled and said, "I have an idea." Weeks later, McCormick began his tour of the Midwest. What he saw convinced him his idea was right. Here were acre after acre of flat, prairie land with no rocks to play tricks on his machines, or hills to tire horses. He left the South for Chicago where he began manufacturing reapers that would soon be rolling over the once deserted plains.

THE FARMERS WHO WATCHED young Cyrus guide his wheat cutting machine in 1831 certainly did not know just how important an invention they were look-

CORBIS-BETTMANN

Farmers could now harvest ten times as much as they could before. (Pictured: an artist's drawing of an early reaper at work.)

a simple machine like that be considered so important?

FOR THOUSANDS OF YEARS the farmers of the world harvested wheat with a large curved knife on the end of a stick called a scythe. A farmer swung the scythe back and forth over and over. For these thousands of years farmers planted only as much wheat as scythes could cut in a week to ten days for that is how long ripened wheat stays good. After a week or so, the ripened wheat rots. It made no sense to plant more wheat than could be harvested.

And then came the McCormick reaper. Farmhands could now harvest ten times as much as they could before! Farmers could plant acres and acres of wheat on the plains of the Midwest and then cut the wheat in the short harvest season. What did all this mean? It meant that less people living on farms could feed more people living in cities. It meant more Americans could leave the farms and work in factories where they could build more locomotives and automobiles and airplanes and a thousand other things.

If we did not have inventions like the reaper, we would spend so much time farming, there would be little time to invent, manufacture, and use all those other wonderful machines.

ing at. Of course, it would help them harvest their own wheat, but was the invention that important?

As inventions go, Cyrus McCormick's reaper was not a complicated machine. In fact, if we compare it to the locomotive or the automobile or the airplane we would have to say that the reaper was really a simple machine. And yet, the invention that Cyrus demonstrated on his neighbor's field that summer day was one of the greatest inventions in the history of the world. How could

1831

Writing Activities

1. GETTING OUT THE WORD

Find the word or words closest to the meaning of the underlined word in each sentence. Then, copy the sentence, using the word or words in place of the underlined word.

1. His <u>calloused</u> hands brushed the dirt away.
   rough skinned   thin   old   scratched up

2. Cyrus began <u>tinkering</u> with his machine.
   painting over   oiling   breaking things   trying different things

3. Cyrus would have to <u>design</u> a new machine.
   build   construct   take apart   plan

4. The breeze <u>rustled</u> the wheat.
   knocked down   swayed   tore   smashed

5. The <u>grizzled</u> farmer yelled out to Cyrus.
   gray haired   experienced   excited   tired

6. He took his place on the <u>rickety</u> seat.
   secure   old   shaky   rusty

7. It was a <u>complicated</u> machine.
   an intricate   simple   fancy   broken down

8. They had to <u>sow</u> the wheat.
   pick up   harvest   plant   protect

2. WHAT'S THE MESSAGE

Copy out the ONE sentence that you think is the story's most important message or idea

A. Farmers work very hard.

B. Wheat is an important crop.

C. Farming is very important.

D. Inventions make life better.

Let's Talk—Discussion Activities

3. THINK IT THROUGH

How would you answer someone who said:

> "You should be willing to invent something to help people and not invent something just to make money."

Take one side or the other:

> It is better to live on a farm than in a city.
>
> It is better to live in a city.

4. TODAY

Think of three or more ways that farming is different from the way it was when Cyrus McCormick was a farmer.

Answer someone who says: "It is a bad idea to invent something that does the work of many people. This puts many people out of work."

5. WHERE'S THE HERO?

What made Cyrus McCormick a hero? Pick out what YOU consider the THREE best answers.

> He was willing to work hard
>
> He made something that helped many other people.
>
> When things went wrong, he did not give up.
>
> He was a good farmer.
>
> He was a good neighbor.

Cooperative Group or Research Activities

6. LOOK IT UP

Select one of the persons listed on the time line for this story. Use other books or articles to gather more information about the person, and then make a presentation explaining why the person might be considered a hero.

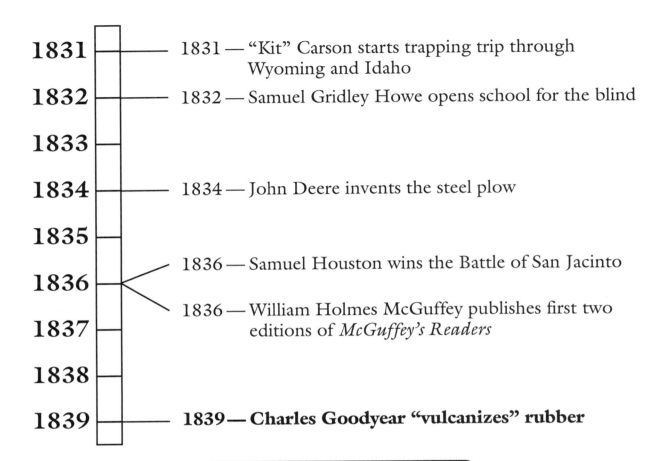

1831 — "Kit" Carson starts trapping trip through Wyoming and Idaho

1832 — Samuel Gridley Howe opens school for the blind

1834 — John Deere invents the steel plow

1836 — Samuel Houston wins the Battle of San Jacinto

1836 — William Holmes McGuffey publishes first two editions of *McGuffey's Readers*

1839 — Charles Goodyear "vulcanizes" rubber

A WORD ABOUT THE STORY

Charles Goodyear
CHEMIST

The problem had never been solved before: How do you take this spongy liquid that flows from a certain kind of tree and turn it into something useful?

Hundreds of people had tried before, but no one had succeeded. What in the world made Charles Goodyear think he could do it? He wasn't even a trained chemist!

The Man Who Never Gave Up

THIN, LANKY 34 YEAR OLD Charles Goodyear walked along the New York sidewalk this late afternoon in 1834 deep in his own thoughts and hardly noticing the darkening sky or the swirling gusts of wind around him. Desperate for money, he had spent the day wandering from one bank to another begging for a loan. Why, he wondered, did every single bank turn him down. Suddenly, a clatter of distant thunder and a torrent of rain interrupted his somber thoughts. Charles scurried to the nearest store in search of shelter.

Once inside, he looked about startled by what he saw. Here were shoes, curtains, coats, boots, curtains, life preservers—familiar things, yet they all looked so strange! The owner noticed Charles's look of surprise.

"Welcome to the Roxbury India Rubber Company," he proudly explained. "Everything you see in the store is made of rubber."

Charles stared in amazement at each item, until his gaze settled on a life preserver. He had just read about a shipwreck where many people had drowned. *Something like this could save lives.* He held up the life preserver and noticed that the valve that let air in and out was badly designed. In an emergency it would take too long to blow up the life preserver.

"I could design a better valve," he told the owner. "Perhaps you will pay me for it." He certainly needed the money. When the owner agreed, Charles dug deep into his pockets, and laid out two dollars and fifty cents for one of the life preservers. On the train trip back to Philadelphia, Charles held the life preserver tightly. After all, he thought, a new design might just keep me from going back to that jail!

A FEW YEARS BEFORE, Charles and his father had opened a hardware store in Philadelphia. At first business was good, but Charles sold goods to customers who promised to pay him later. When times got bad, the customers could not pay their bills. The people who had sold merchandise to Charles demanded their money. Charles owed so much money, however, he could not pay his "creditors" (people you owe money to). In the 1830s, if you did not pay your debts, a creditor could send you to a jail called a "Debtor's Prison." Charles could have kept out of debtors prison by saying he was broke and declaring bankruptcy. However, Charles was very honest; he had studied the Bible and at one time even thought of becoming a minister. "I won't declare bankruptcy," he said. "It's only right that I pay back what I owe." But the truth of the matter was, he could not pay what he owed. He soon found himself behind bars in a small jail. After a few weeks in jail, Charles convinced his creditors to let him out. He would go to New York City, he told them, and ask the banks there to lend him enough money to pay his debts.

WHEN HE RETURNED from New York, Charles explained to his creditors that he did not have the bank loan—but he did have an idea for making money! A few months later, an excited Goodyear took the train back to New York with his newly designed valve. This time he was met by a blistering summer heat wave. Valve in hand, Goodyear rushed to the Roxbury store, headed straight for the owner, and breathlessly began to explain the workings of his wonderful new valve.

The owner interrupted. "Look around you," he shouted. Goodyear looked. The rubber goods the owner had once showed off so proudly were now a sticky goo!

"The valve is not the problem," he shouted. "The gum rubber we use to make the lifeboats—that's the problem. It melts in hot weather! Customers are returning everything we sold them." In fact, he added, the Roxbury India Rubber Company was going out of business. Goodyear was astounded. When Charles asked for some of the gum rubber, the owner gladly gave him a bagful.

A determined Goodyear returned to Philadelphia. In all the years he worked on inventions, he had never felt such a strong yearning to make something work. I will treat or "cure" this gum rubber, he told himself, and make products that people will want. But how? Making things from raw rubber had a long history of failure. Inventors in Europe

Charles Goodyear: He had never felt such a strong yearning to make something work.

and America had been trying to make clothes from rubber for years, but the results were always the same: The clothes were stiff in winter, melted in the summer, and smelled badly.

GOODYEAR KNEW he had to treat or "cure" the raw rubber so that it would stay strong in hot or cold weather. This would not be easy. He had no training in chemistry. He would have to stumble along by trying one thing and then another. Goodyear did have one advantage: Time. Shortly after he returned to Philadelphia, he was thrown into debtors prison again.

A helpful jailer brought him the different items he asked for and he proceeded to mix them with the gum rubber. He tried sand, ink, castor oil, witch hazel, salt, pepper, sugar. Nothing seemed to work. On his release, he went on experimenting in his wife's kitchen. But he needed money—to buy the materials for his experiments, to manufacture rubber products, and to support his wife and children. From time to time, friends and relatives invested money in his idea. When the money ran out—and it always did—he sold what little furniture the family had, pawned his wife's jewelry, and even sold his children's books. When his family did not have enough to eat, neighbors took pity and brought food.

THROUGH IT ALL, Charles remained devoted to his experiments. Nothing would stop him. Once he sold shoes covered with rubber believing he had cured them properly. In time, warm weather ruined them and people demanded their money back. Another time, he boiled the rubber in certain chemicals. The rubber turned firm and smooth. At last, he thought. He sold some clothing made from this cured rubber but soon discovered that when certain foods dripped on the clothes the clothes were ruined.

One failure followed another, until he found a way of mixing the rubber in a certain way with nitric acid. The rubber appeared firm, and not sticky. He received an order to supply 150 mail bags to the U.S. government. *At last!* The 150 bags were manufactured ready for sale to the U.S. Government. All was set—until a sudden heat wave melted them. The people who had invested money with Goodyear were crushed, but Goodyear kept on.

One day, Goodyear accidentally dropped one of the mailbags onto a hot stove. By the time he retrieved the bag, the fire had charred and darkened it. Goodyear poked at the bag.

It was soft and pliable. He left it out in the cold overnight. Instead of being stiff, the mail pouch was still flexible. Goodyear smiled. *At last!* But it would take more money to buy machinery and materials.

The next day Charles met with one of his investors, a friend.

"I have found the answer," he began, "It works!" He held up the flat mail pouch. "I left this rubber bag out all night—in the cold. See—it's still soft, and what's more—"

The investor only shook his head. "Charles, you have been telling me it works for years. And every time you tell me, I believe you, and I invest my money. And then it doesn't work!"

"But this time—" Charles tried to interrupt, but his friend kept on talking. "Your investors keep losing their money. We are not ready to put any more money into making rubber boots and mail bags only to find that the boots melt, the bags get stiff, and they both smell so bad—."

CHARLES WENT EVERYWHERE for more money. No one would listen to him. It would take another *five years* before he could test, patent, find new investors, manufacture, and sell his rubber items. He called his new process for treating rubber "vulcanizing." Thanks to the man who never gave up, "vulcanizing" would change almost every American industry. Americans would soon be wearing rubber clothing, riding on rubber tires, landing airplanes on rubber wheels, and—yes—rescuing people with rubber life preservers that did not melt. And, Charles Goodyear, true to his word, would make enough money to pay off all of his old debts.

1839

Writing Activities

1. GETTING OUT THE WORD

Find the word or words closest to the meaning of the underlined word in each sentence. Then, copy the sentence, using the word or words in place of the underlined word.

1. He was tall and <u>lanky</u>.
   awkwardly thin   heavy   pale   old looking

2. He did not notice the <u>swirling</u> gusts of wind.
   cold   frigid   spinning   fast moving

3. He <u>scurried</u> into the store.
   wandered   slowly walked   scampered   limped

4. Goodyear was <u>astounded</u> by what he saw.
   amused   amazed   entertained   pleased

5. The <u>investors</u> kept losing money.
   buyers   sellers   customers   profit seekers

6. He <u>retrieved</u> the rubber that was in the fire.
   got back   threw out   mixed   whipped up

7. The material was now very <u>pliable</u>.
   firm   hard   flexible   breakable

8. He took care of the <u>debts</u>.
   money he owed   money he saved   money he wanted
   money he earned

2. WHAT'S THE MESSAGE?

Copy out the ONE sentence that you think is the story's most important message or idea.

A. Do not be afraid to give up.

B. It takes money to invent something.

C. Do not let failures keep you from going after your goal.

D. Listen to what other people have to say.

Let's Talk—Discussion Activities

3. THINK IT THROUGH

Charles Goodyear was so busy working on his invention he did not pay enough attention to his wife and children. Should he still be considered a hero?

How do you explain this: Charles Goodyear found a way to "cure" rubber while scientists with more knowledge did not.

4. TODAY

Is it important to pay back money that you owe? Why?

Why do you think we no longer have a debtor's prison in the United States?

5. WHERE'S THE HERO?

What made Charles Goodyear a hero? Pick out what YOU consider the THREE BEST answers.

He was able to get people to invest money in his idea.

He had a good mind.

He paid back the money he owed.

His invention made life better for millions of people.

He had one failure after another, but he never quit.

Cooperative Group or Research Activities

6. LOOK IT UP

Select one of the persons listed on the time line for this story. Use other books or articles to gather more information about the person, and then make a presentation explaining why the person might be considered a hero.

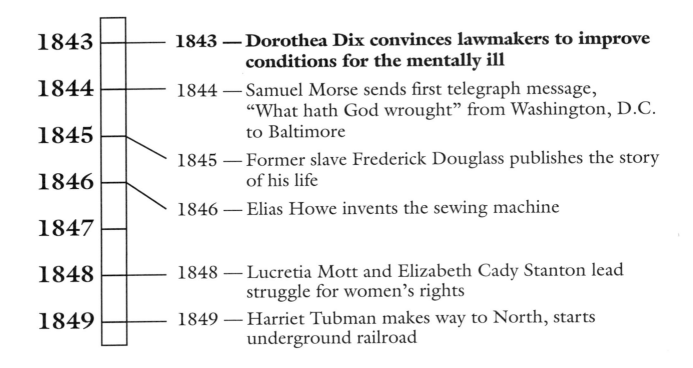

1843 — **Dorothea Dix convinces lawmakers to improve conditions for the mentally ill**

1844 — Samuel Morse sends first telegraph message, "What hath God wrought" from Washington, D.C. to Baltimore

1845 — Former slave Frederick Douglass publishes the story of his life

1846 — Elias Howe invents the sewing machine

1848 — Lucretia Mott and Elizabeth Cady Stanton lead struggle for women's rights

1849 — Harriet Tubman makes way to North, starts underground railroad

A WORD ABOUT THE STORY

Dorothea Dix
REFORMER

Dorothea was horrified by what she saw in the jail that day, but what could she do? Who would pay any attention to a sickly Sunday School teacher—and a woman at that? Then a friend gave Dorothea an idea—an idea that would take up most of her waking hours for the next two years. At the end of the two years, Dorothea felt ready. Would people pay attention now?

She Awakened America

THE JAILER'S WIFE had just taken Dorothea through the small jail. "Do you want to see more?" she asked. Dorothea nodded yes. However, after visiting jails and poorhouses for months, Dorothea believed there was little left to surprise her. She soon discovered how wrong she was.

The woman left Dorothea for a few moments, then returned with a lantern. She held it high as she lead Dorothea to a small stone building behind the jail. As they neared the building, Dorothea noticed that the only way to get in was through a locked iron door. The woman took out a key, slid it into the lock, then slipped the lock from the door.

"Come in," she whispered.

Dorothea followed only to discover a second iron door in front of them. The woman swung the second door open, again inviting Dorothea forward. Dorothea sensed she had entered a room of some sort, but it was too dark to see anything. As Dorothea's eyes tried to pierce the darkness, the woman lifted her lantern. *Oh!* In the flickering light, Dorothy saw a scene that she would remember for the rest of her life. The room was no more than seven feet by seven feet, and perhaps six or seven feet high. A metal frame of some sort laced with a dirty rope stood in the middle of the room. She realized it served as a bed; there was no other furniture in the room. Then, as her eyes grew more accustomed to the dark-

ness, she saw the figure of a man standing near the door. He stood motionless, and uttered not a word. He was draped in filthy ragged clothing, and his feet were bare. Dorothea let out a gasp. She had never seen a man so sad, so thin.

"We keep him locked inside two walls," the jailer's wife explained. "He sometimes, screams and yells so loud — it bothers everyone."

Dorothea took the man's hand, held it in hers, and spoke soft, reassuring words. "We'll get you out of here. I promise." The man stared back through eyes sunk deep in their sockets. Despite the darkness, Dorothea could see tears in his eyes.

Later that night, back in her room, Dorothea gathered her thoughts together. Then, with pen in hand, she wrote with a fury that surprised even her. As her pen scratched across page after page, she remembered more details of what she had seen that day. *I do not want to leave anything out*, she muttered to herself. Just as a warrior of long ago gathered together all his ammunition to prepare for battle, Dorothea was gathering her "ammunition" for a different kind of battle.

DOROTHEA DIX was born in Maine in 1802. Her father came from a well-to-do Boston family, but by the time Dorothea was born, he was a poor farmer, struggling to make ends meet on a farm in Massachusetts. Dorothea felt sad and lonely growing up. When she was 12, she ran off to live with her grandparents in Boston, and later ran off again to live with an aunt. Dorothea was a bright young lady, and, when she grew older, she opened and taught a school for poor children.

Dorothea worked very hard as a teacher. One day she simply collapsed—too tired, too sick, to go on. She probably had tuberculosis—a common lung disease in the 1800's. For the next ten years she fought off her illness. She wrote a few books for children, took a trip to Europe, but by the time Dorothea reached the age of thirty, she was still not well. Once bright, ambitious, and hard-working she felt beaten and defeated. What was she to do?

ONE DAY A MAN at Dorothea's church asked her if she knew of an older woman who would be willing to teach a Bible class at a jail. Dorothea immediately volunteered. "But you are too young," the man protested. Dorothea, however, quickly convinced him that she could take on the task. The following Sunday, Bible in hand, she journeyed to the jail for women in Cambridge, Massachusetts. The lessons went well, but Dorothea noticed three women who always stood away from the others, shivering and huddled together in another room without heat. The other prisoners and the jailer would have nothing to do with them—they were "mentally ill."

Dorothea was horrified. *Why were they in a jail? And why did everyone treat them so poorly?* When she asked the jailer, he retorted: "Nothing I can do. Nothing I want to do."

Dorthea Dix—She awakened America

Dorothea was appalled. She remembered how sad and lonely she had felt growing up.

Nothing he can do? Well, we'll see about that!

The next day, Dorothea told a friend who was an important man in the town what she had seen and heard. "These women lead pathetic lives. They don't belong in a jail," she pleaded. "It is a disgrace. Why don't the lawmakers do something?" She reminded her friend that when she had visited Europe, she had seen places set aside for the mentally ill. "They do so much better when they are treated kindly—instead of like animals."

HER FRIEND LISTENED politely. He knew many of the men who made the laws. "You may be right," he said. "But if you want to convince the lawmakers to make any changes you must have details, facts—solid information. Lots of it. One or two examples are not enough." Impatient by nature, Dorothea was upset by his answer, but realized that her trusted friend was right. She would need the proof. She would have to gather her "ammunition." And so, she set about on a journey that would take her to every jail, every poor house, and every so called work house in the state of Massachusetts. She traveled by stagecoach. The roads in the 1840's were rough and torturous, and often left her exhausted. However, she never slowed down, never gave up. She would visit a place during the day, and that evening sit at a table in her room and write down everything she saw and heard. Her pages of scribbled notes soon filled one notebook after another. Fortunately, Dorothea's grandmother had left some money in her will for Dorothea so she could continue this passion that took up most of her waking hours.

TWO YEARS from the time she began, Dorothea's task was completed. She had visited every single place in the state of Massachusetts that housed the mentally ill. Now she was ready to give the lawmakers the facts—not guesses, not opinions. Dorothy returned to her respected friend with her "ammunition." He looked over the information and promised to see that it came to the attention of the lawmakers.

On a warm June morning in 1843, a member of the Massachusetts state legislature rose to speak. He had in his hand a speech that had been written by Dorothea Dix.

"Gentleman," he began, "I call your attention to the present state of mentally ill persons confined within our state in cages, closets, cellars, stall, pens. They are chained, beaten, and whipped into obedience." The lawmakers sat silently as he described one situation after another: the man who lived alone in the double walled building next to the jail; the wretched housing conditions for women; the man who was placed in a darkened pit with a metal plate placed over the pit so he could not crawl out. "With no heat, no light, little air, he was reduced to frantic cries for help that went unanswered." And on he went...

The lawmakers were shocked. They passed a law: Massachusetts hospitals would have to have a special place for people who were mentally ill. Dorothea had won her battle—but she had no intention of slowing down. Over the next four years Dorothea traveled thousands of miles. From the Atlantic Ocean to the Mississippi River. From the Canadian border to the Gulf of Mexico. By now she was growing famous; she would use her fame to convince lawmakers in other states to pass laws to help the mentally ill. State after state heard her pleas and passed laws similar to the one in Massachusetts.

AS THE 1840s drew to a close, Dorothea Dix believed she had awakened Americans to conditions that had remained hidden too long.

Writing Activities

1. GETTING OUT THE WORD

Copy each sentence. Take out the underlined part and replace it with a word from the ANSWERS. Pick a word that is closest to the meaning of the underlined part.

1. The light <u>flickered</u>.

2. Her eyes grew <u>accustomed</u> to the darkness.

3. He <u>uttered</u> not one word.

4. She <u>assured</u> him by saying that everything would be all right.

ANSWERS:

said	failed	encouraged
reminded	used	went off and on

Do the same for these sentences.

5. She was <u>appalled</u> by what she saw.

6. The women had <u>pathetic</u> lives.

7. Her friend gave a speech before the <u>legislature</u>.

8. They wanted to know the <u>facts</u>.

ANSWERS:

judges	shocked	truth
miserable	exhausted	men who made the laws

2. WHAT'S YOUR CHOICE?

Copy out what you consider to be the three BEST answers.

Dorothea Dix would be a good person to have with you if you—

— were taking an ocean voyage.

— needed a person to help poor people.

— needed a good inventor.

— wanted to change some of the laws.

— needed someone who would not give up easily.

Let's talk—Discussion Activities

3. THINK IT THROUGH

Why do you think some people were so mean to the mentally ill?

Take one side or the other. Explain your answer.

"We should help people who have problems."

"Usually, it is better to let people work out their own problems."

4. WHERE'S THE HERO?

Pick the THREE people on this list that YOU would consider heroes:

A young girl who returns some money she found.

A pilot who makes a difficult landing in an emergency.

A baseball player who hits the winning home run.

A woman who fights to overcome a serious illness

A wonderful singer who entertains many people.

5. WHAT ABOUT YOU?

Did YOU ever help someone else? How did it make you feel?

Cooperative Group or Research Activities

6. LOOK IT UP

Select one of the persons listed on the time line for this story. Use other books or articles to gather more information about the person, and then make a presentation explaining why the person might be considered a hero.

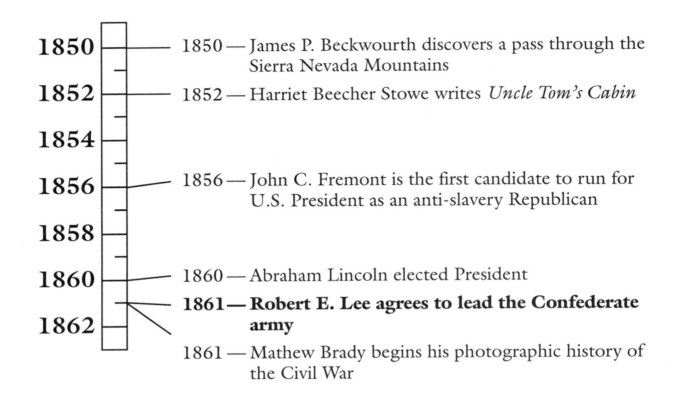

1850 — 1850 — James P. Beckwourth discovers a pass through the Sierra Nevada Mountains

1852 — 1852 — Harriet Beecher Stowe writes *Uncle Tom's Cabin*

1854

1856 — 1856 — John C. Fremont is the first candidate to run for U.S. President as an anti-slavery Republican

1858

1860 — 1860 — Abraham Lincoln elected President

1861 — Robert E. Lee agrees to lead the Confederate army

1862 — 1861 — Mathew Brady begins his photographic history of the Civil War

A WORD ABOUT THE STORY

Robert E. Lee
ARMY GENERAL

Robert E. Lee had to make the most important decision of his life. Should he stay loyal to the Union, or fight on the side of the Confederacy?

Other Americans struggled with this same question in early 1861, but Lee was different — his decision would change the whole course of the war.

The Decision

TALL, HANDSOME U.S. Army colonel Robert E. Lee burst into the family room where his wife sat quietly reading. Mary looked up, startled by her husband's unusual appearance. Ordinarily, he looked so confident and self-assured, but today he appeared upset and very sad.

"Mary," he began, "The news is bad—very bad." He let out a sigh. "Fort Sumter has been bombed!"

For weeks now—ever since he had returned from his Army duty in Texas—Colonel Lee and his wife had been talking about the terrible news in all the Virginia newspapers. After Lincoln was elected President, South Carolina "seceded," or left the Union, saying it was no longer a part of the United States. Later, six more states also seceded. These states claimed that the army forts in their territory no longer belonged to the U.S. President Lincoln, on the other hand, said that no state had the right to secede. He shipped supplies to one of the forts—Fort Sumter in South Carolina. And now, South Carolina had bombed the fort and forced the U.S. soldiers inside to surrender. President Lincoln was calling for 75,000 volunteers to join the Army and put down what he called "the rebellion."

The bombing of the fort meant war!

Mary's eyes swelled up with tears. She looked straight at her husband. "What are you going to do?"

Robert E. Lee shook his head. He understood exactly what she was asking. The states that had left the Union had formed what they called the "Confederate States of America," or the Confederacy. Many U.S. Army officers from the Southern states had left to join the Confederate army; others were staying loyal to the United States, that is, the Union. Lee felt as if he were watching his two best friends circle each other before a terrible fight. What should he do—*Help one side? Help the other? Stay out?*

THE ANSWER came a week later when a messenger arrived at the colonel's home. Colonel Robert E. Lee was to report to General Winfield Scott, the commander of the U.S. Army. When not on duty, Lee lived with his wife and children on a mansion set atop a large rolling hill that overlooked Washington D.C., the nation's capital. Early the next morning, the colonel mounted his favorite horse and rode the short distance to the general's office at the capital. The general must have something important on his mind, he thought.

He was right.

General Scott greeted the colonel warmly. Scott was like a father to the colonel. They had served together in the army for 25 years. The general was a hero who had proved a brave officer both in the war of 1812 and the Mexican War. But he was an old man now—too old to lead an army in battle.

The venerable general took a seat behind his desk. Scott reminded Lee that the President of the United States had called for 75,000 volunteers. Then he paused a moment. Scott remembered how the two

Robert E. Lee would have to make the most important desision of his life.
(Pictured with his horse Traveler)

men had fought together in the war with Mexico. He had watched the way Lee commanded his men. He believed that Robert E. Lee knew how to handle soldiers in battle better than any officer in the army. Scott cleared his throat.

"Lee, I want you to command the Northern army. I know that some Southern officers are leaving the army to fight on the side of the Confederacy," He told Lee. "If you do the same, it will be the greatest mistake of your life."

Back home the next day, Lee shared Scott's offer to command the Northern Army with his wife. By now there was more news—

terrible news. Virginia was about to secede and join the other states of the Confederacy. Lee had hoped with all his heart that Virginia would stay in the Union. Lee's ancestors had arrived in the Virginia colony some two hundred years before. To each Lee generation that followed, Virginia was home. The colonel's father had been a close friend of George Washington. He was once the governor of Virginia. Robert E. Lee's wife, Mary, was the great grand-daughter of President Washington's wife, Martha.

And now, Virginia—the birthplace of presidents George Washington, Thomas Jefferson, James Madison, and James

8

Monroe—was leaving the Union! Lee would now have to make the most important decision of his life. Should he lead the Union Army, or stay loyal to Virginia?

After dinner Lee went upstairs to his bedroom. Mary sat quietly in the family waiting room downstairs. Arthritis had kept her from moving about much, so she spent a good part of the day sitting on a comfortable chair. Now she sat and listened to the familiar footsteps of her husband as he paced the floor above her, deep in his own thoughts.

IN WAR AND IN PEACE, Lee had faithfully served the U.S. Army. He had raised his hand thousands of times and solemnly saluted the flag of the country he loved? *How could he abandon it now? On the other hand, how could he fight against Virginia?*

President Abraham Lincoln said that he would not allow slavery to spread, that a nation could "not remain half slave and half free." Robert E. Lee also believed that slavery was wrong, and had spoken out against it. Like Lincoln, Lee too felt leaving the Union was wrong even though he believed that Northern lawmakers had been unfair to the South. "I can anticipate no greater calamity for the country," he once wrote his son, "than the break up of the Union."

MARY LOOKED UP. The pacing stopped. For a long time all was still. Mary knew what the silence meant. Lee had always been a religious man, and now he knelt in prayer. When he finally stood up, he walked over to his desk and began to write…

Lee came down the stairs well after midnight. He turned to his wife. "I can not see the good of secession," he said slowly, "but how can I draw my sword upon Virginia, my native state?" Mary understood: above all else, Lee believed that his first duty was to defend Virginia. Now, he handed her a note he had written. "I will give this to General Scott tomorrow," he said. As Mary read the lines her eyes filled with tears.

"…I tender my resignation which I request you will recommend for acceptance. It would have been presented at once but for the struggle it has cost me to separate myself from the service to which I have devoted the best years of my life, and all the ability I possessed.

"During the whole of that time—more than a quarter of a century—I have experienced nothing but kindness from my superiors, and a most cordial friendship from my comrades. To no one, General, have I been as much indebted as to yourself for kindness and consideration, and it has always been my ardent desire to merit your approval. I shall carry to the grave the most grateful recollections of your kind consideration, and your name and fame shall always be dear to me.

"Save in the defense of my native state, I never desire again to draw my sword.

"Be pleased to accept my most earnest wishes for the continuance of your happiness and prosperity, and believe me most truly yours. Robert E. Lee."

AFTER HEARING that Lee had resigned, the governor of Virginia asked Lee to head the Virginia army. Lee accepted. He acted out of his sense of love and duty to Virginia, but he did so with a heavy heart. Many Southerners argued that the war would not last long. Lee knew better. He saw a terrible tragedy about to overwhelm both the North and the South. The next four years would show just how right he was.

Writing Activities

1. GETTING OUT THE WORD

Copy each sentence. Take out the underlined part and replace it with a word from the ANSWERS. Pick a word that is closest to the meaning of the underlined part.

1. Mary Lee was <u>startled</u> by her husband's appearance.

2. South Carolina was the first state to <u>secede</u> from the Union.

3. Lincoln wanted to put down what he called a <u>rebellion</u> against the government.

4. The <u>venerable</u> general could not lead the army.

   ANSWERS:

   leave   surprised   revolt
   old and respected   disagreement   soothed

Do the same for these sentences:

5. Lee thought it would be a terrible <u>calamity</u> if Virginia left the Union.

6. She could hear Lee as he <u>paced</u>.

7. Lee decided to <u>resign</u>.

8. Lee said that the other soldiers had always been <u>cordial</u>.

   ANSWERS

   friendly   unpleasant   walked back and forth
   disaster   leave   marched

2. WHAT'S YOUR CHOICE?

Copy out what you consider to be the THREE best answers.

Robert E. Lee would be a good person to have if you —
— needed someone to help you write a book.
— needed someone to help you explore a new land.
— were trying a new science experiment.
— were in a war.
— wanted someone who was loyal.

Let's Talk—Discussion Activities

3. THINK IT THROUGH

How would you answer someone who said: "Lee should not be considered a hero since his side lost the war."

Why was Lincoln against letting the Southern states leave the Union?

4. WHERE'S THE HERO?

Pick the THREE people on this list that YOU would consider heroes:

A policeman who stops a robbery

An artist who paints a beautiful picture

A fireman who rescues a kitten from a tree

A general who wins an important battle for his country

A television actor who entertains many people

5. WHAT ABOUT YOU

What was the most difficult decision YOU ever had to make? How did you feel after you made the decision? Did it turn out to be the right decision?

Cooperative Group or Research Activities

6. LOOK IT UP

Select one of the persons listed on the time line for this story. Use other books or articles to gather more information about the person, and then make a presentation explaining why the person might be considered a hero.

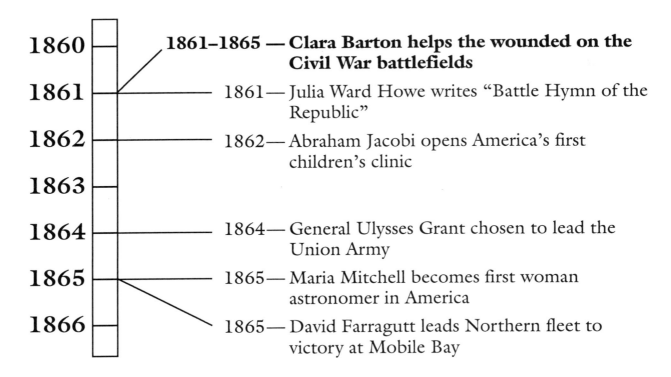

1860	**1861–1865** — **Clara Barton helps the wounded on the Civil War battlefields**
1861	1861— Julia Ward Howe writes "Battle Hymn of the Republic"
1862	1862— Abraham Jacobi opens America's first children's clinic
1863	
1864	1864— General Ulysses Grant chosen to lead the Union Army
1865	1865— Maria Mitchell becomes first woman astronomer in America
1866	1865— David Farragutt leads Northern fleet to victory at Mobile Bay

A WORD ABOUT THE STORY

Clara Barton
NURSE

When the war began, army officers thought of Clara Barton as a "pest." Again and again she brought up the idea of letting women nurses tend the wounded on the battlefields. By war's end, however, soldiers had found another name for her — "Angel of the Battlefield."

Reproduced from the Collections of the LIBRARY OF CONGRESS

Clara Barton—Stubborn lady or "Angel of the Battlefield"?

The Stubborn Lady

"LET ME THROUGH, let me through."

Clara Barton, barely five feet tall, was having trouble jostling her way through the crowd. She pushed and shoved as hard as she could until she reached the edge of the road. Here she stopped and took a deep breath. As far down the road as she could see, army wagons, pulled by panting horses, rolled slowly down the dirt road into Washington, D.C. Clara put her hand to her mouth. Neither the clattering of the wagons, nor their squealing wheels could drown out the terrible sounds of the wounded and dying men on board the wagons. Further down the road, stretching away from the Potomac River, soldiers were taking the wounded out of the wagons and placing them in tents.

Hardly believing what she saw, Clara walked swiftly towards the tents. She spotted a small group of wounded sprawled on the ground. One of them waved a hand, then let it drop. Clara grabbed a cup of water, bent down, and held it to his lips. After a few swallows, he smiled a weak thanks and drifted off to sleep. Clara moved to help another. No one stopped to ask Clara Barton if she were a nurse. In 1861, in all of the United States there were no trained nurses.

News that hundreds of battlefield wounded were returning to Washington, D.C. sent a chill through the capital. No one in the North, it seemed, had expected the Union Army to be defeated—and certainly, no one expected so many dead and wounded. When the Southern states had left or "seceded" from the Union in early 1861, the Southerners declared that they were no longer a part of the United States. President Abraham Lincoln warned them that no state could leave the Union. Whether or not there would be a civil war, he told the Southern Confederates, "was in your hands my dissatisfied fellow countrymen and not mine." Soon afterward, some of the Southern states began taking over U.S. government property in their states. When South Carolina captured Fort Sumter, it became clear to President Lincoln that words were not enough. A Union army would have to force the Southern states back into the Union.

PRESIDENT ABRAHAM LINCOLN called for 75,000 volunteers. Soon thousands of volunteers from the Northern states poured into the nation's capital, and began their military training. Meantime, Washington's citizens assured one another that the war would not last long. "We'll show 'Johnny Reb' a thing or two," one citizen boasted, "And when we do—it will all be over." After months of training, the Northern army was given the order: Seek out and destroy the rebels. On a July day in 1861, thousands of "green," that is, inexperienced soldiers marched out of Washington to the beat of military bands. Citizens lined the streets, waving flags and cheering them on. Northerners told one another that they would

CORBIS-BETTMANN

Now the news was coming back. There were many killed and wounded.
(Pictured: The First Battle of Bull Run)

defeat the rebels and the war would be over in "two, maybe three months."

Now, the news was coming back to Washington. *The battle had been lost!* Northern soldiers were in full retreat. There were many dead and wounded! The terrible truth was sinking in: this would not be a quick, "easy" war. More Northern soldiers would be sent into battle. These soldiers would fight a war far different from any war Americans had ever fought before. By 1861, factories could make many more rifles, more cannon, more mortars, more ships, and more railroad trains than at any time in our history. And of course, many more soldiers would be killed and wounded.

Clara did not think about any of this as she worked late into the night fixing bandages, giving out words of encouragement, and offering food and drink to those wounded or too exhausted to stand. When Clara finally returned to her home that evening, however, she began to mull over what she had seen that day.

SOON CLARA was knocking on the door of a high-ranking army officer. A private tried to talk to her, but she insisted on seeing the officer. When she was finally led in, she wasted no words.

"It is plain to see," she began, "that the wounded men need to be cared for sooner. We can't wait until you bring them back here. It will be too late—many of them will be dead or dying." Clara did not pause. "I want permission to move close to the battlefield so I can care for the wounded there."

The officer looked a little startled. *A woman near the battlefield?* He seemed amused by the idea. "Never!" The officer offered a polite good day to Clara Barton, and assumed that would be the end of that. He did not know just how stubborn Clara could be when it came to helping others…

When Clara was ten years old, her family had what in those days was called a "barn raising." Relatives and neighbors from all around came to help the Barton family put up a new barn. Clara's older brother, David, was on one of the sloping beams of the barn's roof when he slipped and fell to the ground. He was badly injured; doctors did not know if he would live. Little Clara was very close to David, and simply took charge. Over the next two years, a determined Clara spent hour after hour taking care him. No matter how difficult it got, no matter what others said or suggested, Clara stuck to caring for him and nursing him back to health. Meantime the doctors placed worm-like insects called "leeches" on David's body to suck out what doctors claimed was "bad blood." This did more harm than good. It was Clara's care—not the doctor's treatments—that made David well again.

NO, Clara Barton was not the kind of person that stood by when someone needed help. She wrote letters to important people. She knocked on more doors. She persisted for a full year, explaining why it was so important to treat soldiers near the battlefield. Finally, in July of 1862, Clara received a note signed by an important general. "Miss Clara Barton," it began, "has permission to go on the sick transports in any direction—for the purpose of distributing comforts for the sick and wounded and nursing them—always subject to the direction of the surgeon in charge."

AT LAST! Clara had been advertising in newspapers for supplies for wounded soldiers, and had filled a warehouse with the supplies that people had given to her. Now, she loaded up her four mule team wagon with coffee, food, bandages, chloroform and other medical supplies—then headed as close to the battlefield as she dared. A few times, she ventured too close to the enemy, and barely managed to escape capture by scampering away on horseback. There was more to do than she could handle, and so Clara organized a group of women volunteers.

Clara and her volunteers went from one battlefield to another. As soon as the fighting was over, they sought out the wounded. They bandaged their wounds, provided them with fresh clothing, fed them, gave them water, wrote letters to their mothers and loved ones, and covered them with blankets. Doctors agreed that this early care saved many lives.

AFTER THE WAR, people remembered Clara Barton by another name. They called her, "The Angel of the Battlefield." But for Clara, what she had done was not enough. She, and her volunteers, helped the soldiers who had been prisoners of war, nursing them back to health. Later she went to Europe where she served as a nurse for both sides in the Franco-Prussian war. While she was in Europe she saw the work that the international Red Cross did to help wounded soldiers. *Why doesn't America have such an organization,* she wondered. Once back in the U.S. Clara Barton did more than ask that question. She became the driving force that started the American Red Cross.

Writing Activities

1. GETTING OUT THE WORD

Copy each sentence. Take out the underlined part, and replace it with a word from the ANSWERS. Pick a word that is closest to the meaning of the underlined part.

1. Clara Barton <u>jostled</u> her way through the crowd.

2. The soldiers <u>sprawled out</u> on the ground.

3. The Southern states <u>seceded from</u> the United states.

4. The people of the North <u>boasted</u> that they would defeat the Southern army.

ANSWERS:

    bragged   pushed   commented

    left   spread out   claimed

Do the same with these sentences.

5. The Northern army <u>retreated</u> after the battle.

6. Some soldiers were too <u>exhausted</u> to stand.

7. The officer <u>assumed</u> that would be the end of his discussion with Clara Barton.

8. Clara <u>persisted</u> until she got what she wanted.

ANSWERS:

    kept at it   unfamiliar   believed

    fell back   tired   remained

2. WHAT'S YOUR CHOICE?

Copy out what you consider to be the THREE best answers.

Clara Barton would be a good person to have with you if you —

— were injured in an accident.

— were climbing a high mountain.

— went to the park.

— were going to the theater.

— had to convince someone to do something.

Let's Talk—Discussion Activities

3. THINK IT THROUGH

Should we admire or dislike someone who will not take no for an answer? Explain.

Why do you think some people believed it was wrong for women to go near a battlefield?

4. WHERE'S THE HERO

Pick the THREE people on this list that YOU would consider heroes.

A famous football player makes a touchdown to win the game.

A pilot lands a plane safely in nice weather.

A housewife volunteers to help a poor family.

A doctor discovers a cure for a serious illness.

A football player visits some ill children in a hospital.

5. WHAT ABOUT YOU?

Would you like to have someone like Clara Barton for a friend? Explain why or why not.

Did you ever do anything that made you a hero in some way? Explain.

Cooperative Group or Research Activities

6. LOOK IT UP

Select one of the persons listed on the time line for this story. Use other books or articles to gather more information about the person, and then make a presentation explaining why the person might be considered a hero.

1866

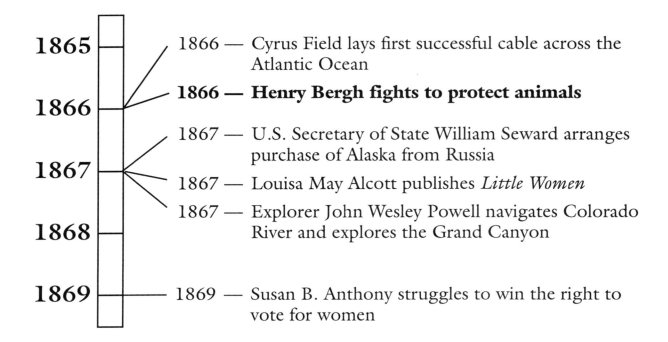

1865

1866 — Cyrus Field lays first successful cable across the Atlantic Ocean

1866 — Henry Bergh fights to protect animals

1866

1867 — U.S. Secretary of State William Seward arranges purchase of Alaska from Russia

1867

1867 — Louisa May Alcott publishes *Little Women*

1867 — Explorer John Wesley Powell navigates Colorado River and explores the Grand Canyon

1868

1869

1869 — Susan B. Anthony struggles to win the right to vote for women

A WORD ABOUT THE STORY

Henry Bergh
HUMANITARIAN

There was nothing in Henry Bergh's early life nor in his appearance to suggest that he might become a hero. In fact, in his early years, Henry had enough money to simply go about enjoying life. Then, amazingly, he changed into a champion "protector," willing to take humiliation and ridicule in order to carry on with what he believed was right.

The man with the thin, sad face was Henry Bergh

10

The "Meddler"

"STOP IT! Stop it, I say!"

The husky man stood on the street beating his reluctant horse with a club when he heard the cry demanding that he stop. *Who in the world was trying to tell him what to do?* The man whirled around.

Standing on the sidewalk was an odd looking, well-dressed man, probably in his fifties. He was tall and gawky, with a thin sad face, and a droopy moustache.

"I say, stop beating that horse," the stranger demanded.

Surprised at first, the husky man soon broke out laughing. "You can't tell me what to do. This is my horse, and I'll do what I want." He lifted the club again and gave the horse another "whomp" on its side. The horse stirred, and as it did, the man jumped on the rickety wagon and grabbed the reins. After all, there was work to be done. It was hard enough trying to make a living in New York City's streets in 1864. Who needed some stranger in fancy clothes telling him what to do?

As the wagon creaked slowly away, the husky man turned around long enough to shout, "Why don't you mind your own business!" By now the few pedestrians on the sidewalk who had stopped to see what the fuss was about began to giggle.

"Mind my own business?" the stranger shouted back. "Treating an animal like that should be everybody's business."

"Yeah," the wagon was moving further away so the man was shouting louder now. "What are you going to do about it?"

The stranger only shook his head. The truth of the matter was there was nothing he could do.

THE MAN with the thin, sad face was Henry Bergh. He was born in New York City in 1813, the son of a wealthy shipbuilder. As he grew up there was little to suggest that Henry Bergh would be anything special—certainly not a hero. He dropped out of college after a few years, deciding that he would rather travel. In time, he inherited a great deal of money from his father. Henry and his wife lived a carefree life of parties, dances, fancy dinners, and travel. When he wasn't going to the theater with his wife, he might be buying paintings for his art collection. One year Henry's travels brought him to London. Here he met the president of a group called the "Royal Society for the Prevention of Cruelty to Animals."

The meeting would change Henry's life forever.

Henry had no deep interest in animals—he had never even owned a pet. Nevertheless, he felt it was very wrong to hurt an animal—any animal—and he was never afraid or embarrassed to speak out when he saw an animal in pain. He told the president of the Royal Society what had happened the year before in New York City. The president seemed surprised. "You mean there was nothing you could do to stop that man from beating his horse?"

"Nothing," Henry answered.

The president explained that in England it was against the law to do such cruel things to animals. In fact, his group had been working to stop cruelty to animals for over forty years. John listened wide eyed as the president went on to say that the Royal Society had the power to stop such terrible things. You could be fined or placed in jail for mistreating an animal.

BACK IN NEW YORK, an inspired Henry Bergh invited a number of important people, including the mayor of the city, to a meeting. Henry was usually a quiet man, but on this day he spoke up and told them some things they would not soon forget.

"Do you know what is going on—right here in New York?" he began. The people in the audience only looked at one another. "Right here, in your fair city, people are pitting one ferocious dog against another. Yes, they are staging dog fights just so they can bet money on who will win!" Henry waited a moment for the audience to quiet down. "I suppose you know that people release pigeons and then shoot at them for sport. But did you know that sometimes they twist a pigeon's wing so that the bird will fly this way and that—to make the shooting more interesting they tell me." Again, Henry waited for the audience to settle down. "I know you see the horses pulling streetcars all over town every day. Did you ever notice just how exhausted they are by the end of the day? Take a look next time, and while you are at it look at that how those leather harnesses cut right into their hides?" Henry did not let up. "The

wild animals in our zoos live in cages so small they can barely move about."

Henry told his audience this was not meant to be just another speech. *Something had to be done.* The cities of England had passed laws to stop this kind of cruelty. Wasn't it time for New York to do the same?

HENRY WON over his audience. In 1866, the New York state legislature passed a law saying that it was illegal, that is, against the law, to hurt an animal on purpose. You could be fined or sent to jail for being cruel to an animal. But that was not all. A new organization called the American Society for the Prevention of Cruelty to Animals was started. The Society had the power to investigate cruelties against animals in New York City and then to present their evidence to a judge. Henry Bergh was elected president of the Society.

The last thing in the world Henry wanted to do was sit back now. From early morning to late at night, he patrolled the streets of New York. New Yorkers soon got used to seeing this gawky figure—always with a top hat, cane, and a badge prominently displayed on his chest—looking in very direction and responding to any complaints of animal cruelty. At first, when Henry saw or heard of someone doing something mean to an animal, he merely spoke to the person and warned him. However, he soon realized people were not taking him seriously. They just went right on being cruel to animals. One day, Henry spied a butcher hauling a wagon full of calves jammed tightly together. They could hardly move. Henry brought the man before a judge who made him pay a fine. The word spread: *Watch out! Henry Bergh meant business.*

Many people, however, still thought of Bergh as a silly old man. Some threw rotten food at him as he made his rounds, or heckled him with nasty words. One man even tried to hit him with a metal rod. Newspapers delighted in running cartoons that showed him as a thin, long nosed, busy-body who "meddled" in other people's business. One newspaper gave him the nick-name, "The Meddler,"—and the name stuck. The ridicule and humiliation bothered Henry, but he answered with courage and dignity. Not for a moment would he give up

Newspapers delighted in running cartoons that poked fun at Henry Bergh

what now became his life's work! And so, Henry went about patrolling the streets, raising money, giving much of his own money, building animal shelters, buying ambulance wagons for mistreated animals, or hauling an offender off to see a judge. Little by little, Henry thought he began to see a wonderful thing beginning to happen—*weren't more people acting kinder to animals now?*.

Other people volunteered to help. With Henry leading the way, a group of these volunteers "made the rounds." One day they would break up a dog fight, and Henry would shame the watching spectators. Another day, the volunteers would stop an overloaded rail streetcar, and Henry would demand that some of the people get off before he would allow the overworked horses to continue. Sometimes they rescued dogs or cats trapped in trees or buildings. Henry even had a special harness built to lift horses that had fallen in deep ditches.

Henry Bergh's idea of being kind to animals spread swiftly to other cities. He gave speeches; he offered suggestions. He saw to it that young children in schools were taught to be kind to animals. With Henry serving as the spirit and guiding light, people in hundreds of cities all over the United States started their own Societies for the Prevention of Cruelty to Animals. For the next 22 years—until his death in 1888—Henry devoted his strength and his life to winning people over to treating animals properly.

BY THE TIME Henry died, the same newspapers that had once made fun of "The Meddler," gave him their warmest respect. They reminded their readers how he had fought so hard for what he believed in, how he had never given up.

Henry Bergh had replaced cruelty with kindness.

Writing Activities

1. GETTING OUT THE WORD

Copy each sentence. Take out the underlined part and replace it with a word from the ANSWERS. Pick a word that is closest to the meaning of the underlined part.

1. The horse appeared <u>reluctant</u> to move.

2. He was <u>gawky</u>.

3. <u>Pedestrians</u> stopped to watch.

4. He <u>inherited</u> money when his father died.

   ANSWERS:

received	unwilling	awkward looking
graceful	spectators	people walking along

Do the same with these sentences.

5. It was now <u>illegal</u> to hurt an animal on purpose.

6. Some people said that John Bergh was <u>a meddler</u>.

7. The newspapers made fun of and <u>humiliated</u> him.

8. He sometimes took an <u>offender</u> to a judge.

   ANSWERS:

embarrassed	beneficial	someone who broke the law
a policeman	against the law	someone who interferes

2. WHAT'S YOUR CHOICE?

Copy out what you consider to be the THREE best answers.

Henry Bergh would be a good person to have with you if you —

— needed someone to take care of your pet.

— wanted to convince other people to do something.

— needed someone to take care of your garden.

— wanted someone to fly an airplane.

— wanted to start a new organization or club.

#10

Let's Talk—Discussion Activities

3. THINK IT THROUGH

Take one side or the other. Explain your answer.

"It should be against the law to make fun of someone in the newspapers or on television."

"You should be able to make fun of anyone in the newspapers or on television."

4. WHERE'S THE HERO?

Pick the THREE people on this list that YOU would consider heroes:

A fireman who saves someone from a burning building.

A pilot who delivers food to people lost in a storm.

Someone who finds a new job.

A fireman who rescues a kitten in a tree.

A scientist who discovers a cure for a disease.

5. WHAT ABOUT YOU?

Did you ever see an animal mistreated? How did you feel?
What did you do?

Cooperative Group or Research Activities

6. LOOK IT UP

Select one of the persons listed on the time line for this story. Use other books or articles to gather more information about the person, and then make a presentation explaining why the person might be considered a hero.

1871	1871 — Simon Ingersoll invents a pneumatic drill
1872	
1873	1873 — Joseph Glidden's invention of barbed wire makes it possible for small farmers to settle the frontier
1874	
1875	
1876	1876 — Alexander Graham Bell invents the telephone
1877	**1877 — Chief Joseph surrenders**
1878	1878 — Albert Michelson measures the speed of light
1879	1879 — Thomas Edison invents the electric light

A WORD ABOUT THE STORY

Chief Joseph
INDIAN CHIEF

When the U.S. government ordered Chief Joseph and his band of Indians to leave their land and move to a small area, Joseph was stunned. He answered, "You might as well expect the rivers to run uphill as to expect that a man who was born free should be content to be penned up and denied liberty." When the government still insisted that he move his tribe, Joseph and his band of Indians set out on an escape journey that defies belief.

"I Will Fight No More Forever"

CHIEF JOSEPH'S FACE WAS SAD. The words he spoke came from a heavy heart as his weary body leaned into the icy Montana wind that whipped across the snow covered plain. His lips moved slowly, but he stood tall and straight, this proud Indian chief. He had come under a white flag of truce to surrender.

"I am tired of the fighting," he told the U.S. Army colonel. "Our chiefs are killed....The old men are all dead. He who led the young men is dead. It is cold and we have no blankets. The little children are freezing to death. My people have no food. I want to have time to look for my children and see how many of them I can find. Maybe I shall find them among the dead. Hear me, my chiefs, my heart is sick and sad. From where the sun now stands, I will fight no more forever."

With these words Chief Joseph ended one of the most remarkable journeys in history.

For hundreds of years—even before there was a United States—bands of Nez Perce (pronounced Nez Purse) Indians had lived on the beautiful land that stretched across northeast Oregon. They called this lush country Wallowa— Land of the Winding Waters. Here they grazed cattle, raised horses, gathered berries, and hunted and fished. This was their home, their land! Then in the middle 1800s settlers began passing through the Wallowa Valley on their way to the land that lay further west. The Nez Perce Indians did not mind seeing the wagons rolling across their land—as long as they continued moving west.

In the early 1870s all of this changed. *The settlers were not moving on!* They were finding places in the Wallowa Valley to settle and call home. Here they built cabins and fences, farmed, grazed their animals—all on Indian land. The soil was rich—perfect for farming. The country was beautiful, with rolling hills surrounded by mountains and canyons. Here too were lakes and creeks with clear running water, and trees for lumber—and even gold.

The settlers worked very hard, and felt they did no wrong—but this could only mean trouble.

THE U.S. GOVERNMENT had agreed that the Wallowa Valley was Indian territory. Settlers were not supposed to be there. The Indians complained, but the U.S. government did not tell the settlers to leave. Instead, U.S. officials cut back the amount of land set aside for the Indians. "After all you only wander about gathering roots and berries or hunting," they told the Indians.

1877

"The settlers are farming and building homes."

Chief Joseph became the leader of one of the bands of Nez Perce Indians when his father died in 1870. Joseph's Indian name meant "Thunder Rolling Down From The Mountains," but he was a gentle, caring man. He stood six feet tall, and though he was young for a chief, the Indians had learned to respect and admire his calm, dignified manner. Joseph was a man of peace, proud that he had never killed a man. The young warriors wanted to go to war and drive the settlers out, but Chief Joseph told them he would not go to war. Instead, he met with the government officials.

"Our father and our father's father, and his father, too, lived on these lands." he explained to the officials. "They are buried here. To ask that we give up our land is like asking us to give up our parents."

Chief Joseph swept his arm across a wide arch. "This land is ours."

THE GOVERNMENT OFFICIALS would not listen. More settlers arrived each year, and the officials kept cutting back the Indian land. Finally, on a June day in 1877, the U.S. government told the Nez Perce Indians: "You must leave this land and take your families to a place we have set aside for you—a 'reservation' in Idaho."

Chief Joseph was shocked. He refused to sign any agreement or treaty. He told the officials, "You might as well expect the rivers to run backward as to expect that a man who was born free should be content to be penned up and denied liberty." It did not matter—the Indians would have to move off their land. Chief Joseph went to the U.S. Army general whose army was ready to force the Indians off the land. Unlike Chief Joseph, General Howard had been in many battles. In one of the battles during the Civil war, he had lost an arm. He wanted the Indians to leave peacefully for their new land.

The young warriors wanted to stay and fight. *How would they fish and hunt in such a tiny place? How could they be free if they had to stay in one place?* Chief Joseph listened, but he reminded the warriors that the U.S. Army had many more men. "Most of you have only bows and arrows," he said. "The army has rifles and cannons. It will be like the deer fighting the bear." No, Joseph did not want any fighting.

BUT IT WAS NOT TO BE. In a few cruel moments, a settler killed an Indian, and three Indians killed four settlers. "I would have given my own life," Chief Joseph said, "If I could have undone the killing of the settlers." Now there would be no peace.

Some 500 Nez Perce Indians—old men, women and children—together with their horses and some 250 warriors set out on a journey that they hoped would lead them to Canada and freedom. They knew that if they stayed in one place too long, the soldiers would overtake them. And so, they hid in the mountains, moved through the gullies, and around canyons. Whenever the army caught up with them, the warriors fought back while the women and children hid. After the battles, they buried the dead, loaded the wounded on horses—and moved on. They traveled from Oregon to Idaho and then into Montana.

Finally, on an October morning, what remained of the Indian band reached Bear Paws Mountains. They were forty miles from Canada and freedom! The women and children, however, were too exhausted to move on. They stopped to rest between two hills that sheltered them from the biting wind. The Nez Perce warriors believed that the soldiers were still far behind them—they were wrong. Early the next morning the U.S. Cavalry—some six hundred soldiers—swooped down on them. Surprised, the warriors fought back. As the battle raged, Chief Joseph and his braves knew they could escape and move on to Canada—but it would have meant leaving the exhausted women, and children behind. And so they stayed and fought. By the fifth day, Chief Joseph knew that all was lost.

SINCE LEAVING THEIR home, the Indians had journeyed 1400 miles, fought six battles, and somehow managed to hold off the the pursuing soldiers for 111 days. Now, it was over. Chief Joseph came forward to say, "From where the sun now stands, I will fight no more forever." True to his word, Chief Joseph never fought again.

Chief Joseph: "You might as well expect the rivers to run uphill as to expect that a man who was born free should be content to be penned up and denied liberty."

Writing Activities

1 GETTING OUT THE WORD

Copy each sentence. Take out the underlined part and replace it with a word from the ANSWERS. Pick a word that is closest to the meaning of the underlined part.

1. His body was <u>weary</u> after walking all day.

2. The women and children were too <u>exhausted</u> to move on.

3. The cattle were left to <u>graze</u>.

4. The hills <u>sheltered</u> them.

ANSWERS:

find food	worn out	protected
rest	tired	harmed

Do the same for these sentences

1. They got water from the <u>creek</u> nearby.

2. The Indians admired his <u>dignified</u> manner.

3. They moved through the <u>gully</u>.

4 The <u>cavalry</u> followed them.

ANSWERS:

foot soldiers	stream	large ditch
quiet	distinguished	soldiers on horses

2. WHAT'S YOUR CHOICE

Copy out what you consider to be the THREE best answers.

Chief Joseph would be a good person to have if you—

— were going on a camping trip.

— were exploring a new land.

— were trying to solve a math problem.

— were eager to start a fight.

— were trying to settle an argument.

Let's Talk—Discussion Activities

3. THINK IT THROUGH

If YOU were an Indian, would you want to placed on a reservation? Explain your answer.

Take one side or the other. Explain your answer.

"The settlers had good reasons to take more land from the Indians."

"The settlers were wrong in taking more land from the Indians."

Explain this: Even though Chief Joseph failed to do what he set out to do, people still consider him a hero.

4. WHERE'S THE HERO?

Pick the THREE people on this list that YOU would consider heroes.

A student who likes to read

A citizen who votes in every election

A pilot who brings food and supplies to people lost in a storm

A lifeguard who saves someone from drowning

A baseball player who hits his fiftieth home run

5. WHAT ABOUT YOU?

How would you feel if you and your family had to move far away to another part of the country this week?

Cooperative Group or Research Activities

6. LOOK IT UP

Select one of the persons listed on the time line for this story. Use other books or articles to gather more information about the person, and then make a presentation explaining why the person might be considered a hero.

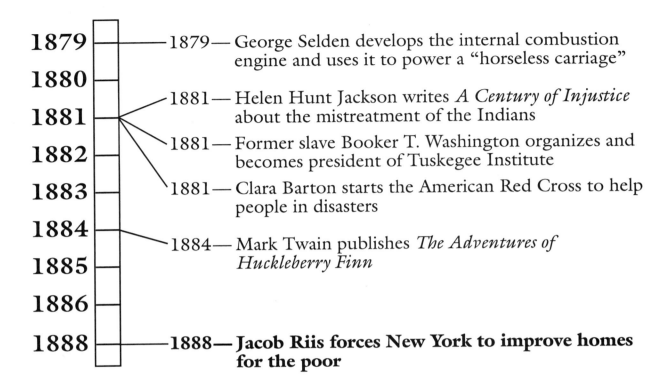

1879 — George Selden develops the internal combustion engine and uses it to power a "horseless carriage"

1881 — Helen Hunt Jackson writes *A Century of Injustice* about the mistreatment of the Indians

1881 — Former slave Booker T. Washington organizes and becomes president of Tuskegee Institute

1881 — Clara Barton starts the American Red Cross to help people in disasters

1884 — Mark Twain publishes *The Adventures of Huckleberry Finn*

1888 — **Jacob Riis forces New York to improve homes for the poor**

A WORD ABOUT THE STORY

Jacob Riis
JOURNALIST

When a young Jacob Riis first stepped off the ship that brought him to America, his only thought was to find work. He drifted from one difficult job to another. He could not help but notice how long and hard Americans worked. In time, Jacob became a writer for a newspaper. Now, he could forget about his own back-breaking work experience and the laborers he left behind. Or could he?

Man with a Mission

WHEN OUR COUNTRY BEGAN, Americans were making the things they needed with their hands. By the 1870s and 1880s all of this changed. Machines in large factories made most of the products Americans used. This change, called the "Industrial Revolution," gave Americans many wonderful things and gave them millions of jobs. It made America a prosperous nation. But the Industrial Revolution also created some serious problems. Some American writers began writing about these problems. One writer, for example, described life in the coal mines in Pennsylvaniaç

The ragged looking boys sit in rows working in the "coal breaker" room. The room is in a building that looks like a shed located near the coal mine. It is a large room—about 20 feet wide by 20 feet long. The boys sit above six boards that cross the room. In a room above, heavy machinery crushes the coal and then a stream of the crushed coal slides down the boards to the boys. As the black coal passes, each boy's fingers search out bits of slate from the coal. Some of the boys are 8 or 9, others 10 or 11. Almost all of them are small for their ages. Their fingers have many cuts from picking out the slate, and they cough from time to time from the coal dust that is everywhere. They sit hunched over, and work in gloomy silence. Even if they wanted to talk, the noise of the sliding coal would drown out their words. With the slate removed, the coal will burn hotter and cleaner—*but at what cost?* The boys start at seven in the morning. Except for a short time off for lunch, they work until dark—ten or twelve hours. Each boy sees the same picture: the endless line of coal; the dirty, unsmiling faces of the other boys; the dust and grime. *What is it like to laugh? To play? What is reading and writing? What is school? Don't ask these boys. They sit in gloomy silence.*

Another writer told about life in the textile mills in New England...

The "bobbin boy" starts his work before dawn. He is seven, or eight, or nine. He stands in the dim light next to the giant, noisy machines that weave thread into cloth. The lint in the air makes his eyes burn and his throat dry. Always, he keeps his eyes on the many wooden spools of thread, called "bobbins," that feed the looms. When a thread breaks, or a bobbin runs out of thread, he quickly clambers bare footed up the machine with another spool. He is careful—very careful. He does not want his arms or legs getting tangled in the whirling machines. After he changes the bobbin, he works his way to the floor, then stares again at the bobbins above. At the same time, little girls just as young, stand alongside their mothers helping them tend machines that turn thread to cloth. All will work ten or twelve hours a day.

Another described a small boy working in a New Jersey factory that made glass bottles...

The young boy grips the long handled flat shovel firmly, slides it under the bottle, then lifts it from the coal burning furnace. He knows not to look straight inside—the fire appears as bright as the sun. And he knows to be careful as he carries the bottle to the workmen. If a bottle drops, it shatters, sending fiery shards of glass everywhere. The boy swelters in the heat, but there will be no slowing down. Each factory is interested in speed, in getting out as many products as they can.

The writers who described these problems and wanted things to change were called "reformers." One of the best know American reformers was Jacob Riis...

A WIDE-EYED JACOB RIIS stepped off the ship docked in New York harbor on an early Sunday morning in 1870. Jacob was twenty, and had spent the last four years learning how to be a carpenter in Denmark, his native land. He had decided to bring his carpenter skills to America—the land of opportunity.

Jacob was in for a terrible disappointment. He wandered the streets of New York for weeks in search of work as a carpenter with little luck. No matter, he thought. He would

Jacob Riis: He never forgot what it was like to be poor.

take any kind of job. Jacob drifted from New York, to Pennsylvania, to New Jersey, then back to New York, barely making enough to live on. He worked on a farm; he dug coal in a coal mine; he labored in a brick making factory; he peddled on the streets; he cut ice; he chopped trees. And when there was no work, and no money, he slept in dank basement "shelters" set up for the poor.

ONE DAY, JACOB HEARD about a job at a weekly newspaper. Back in Denmark, Jacob had helped his father who wrote for a small newspaper. He wrote well, and his father had taught Jacob many subjects at home. He applied for the newspaper job and was hired. Once he started, Jacob knew this was the work he wanted to do for the rest of his life. He went on to work for other small newspapers, and then in 1877—seven years after he had stepped off the ship—Jacob Riis was working as a full time reporter for a very important New York newspaper.

Jacob never forget how poor he once was. He knew what it was like to wander the streets dejected and hungry. He began to write stories about the poor, forgotten people who lived in New York's east side. He painted pictures with his words. He told of streets teeming with thousands of people. He described the dingy, overcrowded apartments they lived in—stifling hot in summer, and poorly heated in the winter. He told about the small, dirty children who wandered the streets and alleys, and how they played in the streets because there were no playgrounds. And, of course, he described the work at home:

> "A father brings home bundles of unfinished pants, blouses, shirts, hats, dresses, sweaters. After supper, the garments are spread out. Mother and father begin to sew. The children's tiny fingers grow busy too—making artificial flowers, sorting feathers, sewing buttons, gathering hems, stitching threads on cloth that show mother and father where to sew. The pay will be small, the heat will grow more stifling, but on the family works into the wee hours of the night. The family needs the money to pay the rent and to buy food…"

JACOB WANTED TO DO MORE than tell a story. He loved America very much. He believed he had a mission to tell other Americans about the poor so that conditions would improve. He knew that the children he saw wandering in the streets, or working hour after hour were America's future citizens. If we want our children to become good citizens, he told his readers, we must stop child labor and educate our children. *Let's build more schools, more playgrounds, more parks. Let's tear down houses not fit to live in.*

One morning, Jacob Riis sat reading his morning paper over a cup of coffee when a news article caught his eye. Someone in Europe had invented a "flash" so that a camera could take pictures in the dark! Jacob was excited by what he read. In a short time, he had a flash to go with his camera. Now he could go into the poorly lighted, dingy places where the poor lived at night, when life was even gloomier. Jacob's newspaper began printing his photos along with his stories. Now, Jacob realized, his message would be more than just words.

Jacob Riis and other reformers began to influence the way Americans felt. In time, different laws were passed: A worker could only work so many hours. Factories had to be safe. Dilapidated, unsafe buildings had to be repaired or torn down. And, most important of all, child labor was stopped. Jacob Riis was proud of the part he played in making America a better country.

Writing Activities

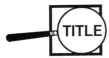

1. FIND THE TITLE

Copy out what you think is the best title for this story:

The Carpenter Who Became Famous

The Man Who Made a Difference

Traveling Man

The Story of an Honest Man

2. GET THE PICTURE

You are painting some scenes to illustrate the life of Jacob Riis. Pick out the THREE scenes that BEST describe him.

Riis writing at a desk   Riis painting a picture

Riis riding in a limousine   Riis with a camera

Riis visiting a poor home   Riis tramping in the forest

3. IMAGINE

A time machine takes you back in time and you meet Jacob Riis. What three questions would you ask him?

Imagine you are Jacob Riis. Someone asks you, "Why did you make such a fuss over poor people? Wouldn't it be easier for you if you did not?" How would you answer the person?

Imagine that you are describing Jacob Riis to a friend. Pick out the FOUR words that you would most likely use.

caring   egotistical   miserly   sensitive

boastful   compassionate   sympathetic   callous

Imagine that you are a writer working for a newspaper today. What problems would you choose to write about?

Let's Talk—Discussion Activities

4. TAKE A SIDE

Jacob Riis wanted the government to help the poor people in the city. Take one side or the other, and then give all the reasons you can for the side you take.

"The government should do all it can to help poor people."

"The government should do little to help the poor. Poor people will do better without the help of government."

5. FIND AN ANSWER

Why do many people think that Jacob Riis was a hero?

Jacob Riis had a difficult time when he first arrived in America. Do you think this influenced what he wrote about? How are people influenced by the things that happen to them?

Would you rather:

— spend your time helping others or spend your time working to get rich and famous?
— travel around the world or work at a job you like to do?
— have a friend describe you as "generous" or descibe you as "courageous?"
— overhear someone compliment you on the way you look or compliment you on the good things you do?

Cooperative Group or Research Activities

6. LOOK IT UP

Select one of the persons listed on the time line for this story. Use other books or articles to gather more information about the person, and then make a presentation explaining why the person might be considered a hero.

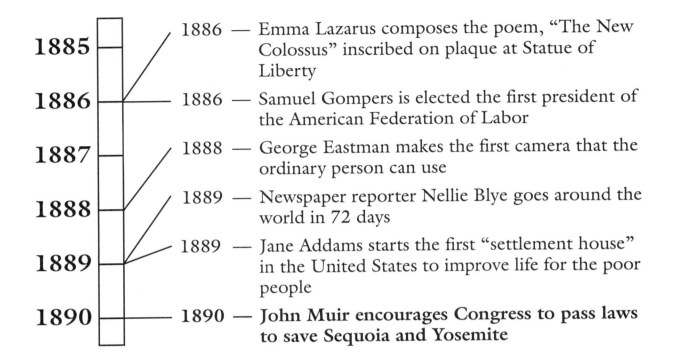

1885

1886

1887

1888

1889

1890

1886 — Emma Lazarus composes the poem, "The New Colossus" inscribed on plaque at Statue of Liberty

1886 — Samuel Gompers is elected the first president of the American Federation of Labor

1888 — George Eastman makes the first camera that the ordinary person can use

1889 — Newspaper reporter Nellie Blye goes around the world in 72 days

1889 — Jane Addams starts the first "settlement house" in the United States to improve life for the poor people

1890 — **John Muir encourages Congress to pass laws to save Sequoia and Yosemite**

A WORD ABOUT THE STORY

John Muir
NATURALIST

He had no regular job, owned no factory, held no political office. In fact, he called himself "a tramp" and spent most of his time just wandering about. Yet, when he urged Americans to save their most valuable treasures, they listened!

#13

"The Tramp"

JOHN FELT THE STABBING PAIN the instant the metal hit his eyes.

"I can't see," he yelled. "I can't see."

The other workers at the wagon factory rushed over to help, but there was really nothing they could do. The thin metal file that John had been using to pry loose a large factory belt had flipped back and hit him across the eyes.

Later that day a doctor told John that he might never see again. For the next month John sat in a darkened room at home, living through a terrible nightmare that had taken over his life. These were awful days—and worse nights—for a man still in his twenties, but John did not complain. He had faced difficult times before...

JOHN MUIR was born in Scotland in 1838. His parents were poor; his father made barely enough to feed the family. Little John went to a strict school where students studied Latin and French as well as English. If a teacher thought a student did not study hard enough, he would hit the student with a leather strap. In 1841 John's family came to America. Later they settled on a plot of land in southern Wisconsin, and here his father set about building a log cabin, and clearing the unbroken soil for farming. John's father had little understanding of children. Though John was but eleven—and his brother a few years younger—he demanded that they work as long and as hard as any strong, full-grown men.

John awakened each morning before dawn to sharpen the farm tools, feed the animals, chop wood for the stove, and carry water up the hill from the spring. After a hastily eaten breakfast, he spent the rest of the day splitting rails, laying fences, caring for the animals, and plowing or cutting grain. And when day was done, and he had eaten dinner, and said his prayers, and felt about as tired as it was possible for anyone to feel—it was time for bed. John loved to read, but there was no time for anything but work. In fact, his father allowed him and his brother but two days off the entire year.

One day, John asked his father if he could take part of the day off. "I want some time to read," he explained.

His father laughed. "You want to read?" he scoffed. "You'll get no time off from work! If you want to read, get up a little earlier."

John followed his father's suggestion, though it was not exactly what his father had in mind. John awakened at one each morning, and read until just before dawn. He soon discovered that he could get along with but five hours of sleep. John kept working on his father's farm until he was 21 when he decided to go to college. Though he had not been to school since he was eleven years old, John convinced the officials at Wisconsin University to let him enroll. He was a good student, but he also had to work at different jobs to earn enough for food. John liked college, but after a few years, he wanted to do more. "Books are all right," he told his friends, "but I want to travel, to see things." He added that he was "leaving the University

John Muir: His love of nature drove him on

of Wisconsin for the University of the Wilderness."

Ever since John was a small boy back in Scotland, he was fascinated by the wilderness. He loved to listen to the birds sing, or roam the seashore in search of shells and seaweeds. If he saw a sparrow's nest or a sprouting seed or a blooming flower, he stared in rapt attention. He seemed caught up by nature's beauty, and as he grew older this deep love for nature only grew stronger.

After John left the university, he wandered on foot through Wisconsin, Iowa, and then north through parts of Canada. By now he had an even deeper respect and understanding for the flowers, the trees, the mountains, and the glaciers for he had studied chemistry, and physics, and botany (the study of plants) at the university.

Back from his wanderings, John went to work at a carriage factory in Minneapolis. He still felt close to nature, but he knew he had to make a living. John had always been a highly skilled inventor and craftsman. He could take bits of metal or wood and fashion them into tools, thermometers, water wheels, or special clocks that told time and the day of the week. He even invented a bed that tipped straight up at a certain set time, pushing the occupant out of bed. The factory owner was quick to recognize John's skills and set him to work on a machine that made hubs and spokes for carriages. All went well—until the day of the terrible accident...

FOR THE FIRST FEW DAYS John sat in his darkened room, hardly knowing what to think. "My days were terrible beyond what I can tell, and my nights were if possible more terrible," he later admitted. In the darkness, he recalled how much he loved inventing things. But he also remembered how thrilled he felt hiking across the land. If I get my sight back, John wondered, should I spend my life inventing things, or studying nature?

Little by little, over the next 30 days, John Muir's eyesight returned. Now, the factory owner urged John to return to inventing. "If you do," he confidently told John, "You will be a rich man some day." But John had already made his decision: He would spend the rest of his life drifting about studying what he called,"the inventions of God." Years later, he would say, "I could have been a millionaire, but I decided to be a tramp."

Once he felt well, John decided to hike from the southern tip of Indiana, down through the Southern states. When friends asked what route he planned to take, he simply answered: "Oh, anywhere in the wilderness." Once on the trail, John avoided towns or cities, or any other places where large numbers of people might be. He chose instead to tramp through woods and underbrush, to explore deep caverns and to clamor up a mountain peak, or cross a winding river to reach a tumbling waterfall.

On he walked—through Kentucky, Tennessee and Georgia, and then across Florida to the Gulf of Mexico. Throughout the journey he kept a "journal." In it, he made sketches of what he saw and described his excitement and exhilaration on seeing the many wonders of nature. He carried a "plant press" that he used like a vice to press and preserve hundreds of plants and flowers.

By journey's end, he had walked 1,000 miles!

JOHN MUIR'S WANDERINGS were far from over. He boarded a boat to Panama, crossed the isthmus, and sailed to San Francisco. But he wanted no part of city life. "I want to go to any place that is wild," he said. Soon he was wandering across California's Central Valley, exulting over the beautiful wild flowers that blossomed as far as the eye could see. On he hiked—to the rugged Sierra Nevada Mountains. Then he began to climb, higher and higher, until he came upon a scene of beauty that took his breath away—the Yosemite Valley. He described Yosemite—with its majestic mountains, crystal-like rivers, enormous rocks, and cascading waterfalls—as a large temple lighted from above where "nature had gathered her choicest (best) treasures."

John Muir's love of nature drove him on. Whether it was the mountains and glaciers of Alaska or the petrified forests of Arizona or the redwoods of California he remained as excited by nature as he was as a small boy in Scotland. In search of more wilderness, he took trips to Africa, India, Siberia, Australia, South America, and New Zealand.

SOMEONE ONCE ASKED John Muir what he did. "Oh," he answered, "I'm just a tramp." He was, of course, so much more. He was, in fact, an explorer, a champion walker, a scientist, and an author who became one of the most popular and well known persons in America. He wrote and spoke out about how important it was to save, or conserve, the trees, the rivers, the waterfalls, the forests so that our children and grandchildren could also enjoy the wonders of nature.

What he said and what he wrote made sense to Americans—and to Congressmen and U.S. presidents as well. In 1890, laws were passed to protect our forests, and to set aside and protect large areas of the wildness that were to be called our "National Parks."

TODAY, THE MILLIONS of Americans who visit and enjoy the wonderful sights of America's National Parks can thank that little boy from Scotland who devoted his life to the wonders of nature.

Writing activities

1. FIND THE TITLE

Copy out what you think is the best title for this story:

The Man Who Loved the Outdoors

The Beauty of the Outdoors

The Man Who Became Famous

The Story of Yosemite

2. GET THE PICTURE

You are painting some scenes to illustrate the life of John Muir. Pick out the THREE scenes that BEST describe him.

Muir studying some plants   Muir tramping through the woods

Muir living in an apartment   Muir driving an auto

Muir writing   Muir shopping in a store

3. IMAGINE

Imagine that you are John Muir, and you keep a diary. Write how you feel when you:

— can see again.

— start on your first long hike.

— see Yosemite Valley for the first time.

Imagine that someone just came here from Mars and does not know anything about the earth's natural resources. The Martian looks at you quizzically and asks why you bother to protect the earth's natural resources from harm. Give your answer by copying and completing each of these sentences.

1. Trees are important to me because _____.

2. Rivers are important to me because _____.

3. Plants are important to me because _____.

4. Flowers are important to me because _____.

5. Rich soil is important to me because _____.

#13

Let's Talk—Discussion Activities

4. TAKE A SIDE

Sometimes when we save trees or other natural resources, factories can not get all the materials they need. Take one side or the other, and then give all the reasons you can for the side you take.

"Saving our natural resources is more important than making more things in our factories."

"Giving people jobs in factories is more important than saving trees or other natural resources."

Many people are very concerned that certain animals will die off (become extinct) if we do not protect them. Take one side or the other, and then give all the reasons you can for the side you take.

"We should do all we can to protect animals such as elephants and tigers from dying off."

"It does not matter if some animals become extinct. It's more important that we spend our time helping people."

5. FIND AN ANSWER

Imagine you are John Muir. Someone asks you: "Why didn't you take that job in the factory? You could have been rich." How would you answer?

Does John Muir remind you of anyone you know or read about?

Cooperative Group or Research Activities

6. LOOK IT UP

Select one of the persons listed on the time line for this story. Use other books or articles to gather more information about the person, and then make a presentation explaining why the person might be considered a hero.

1899

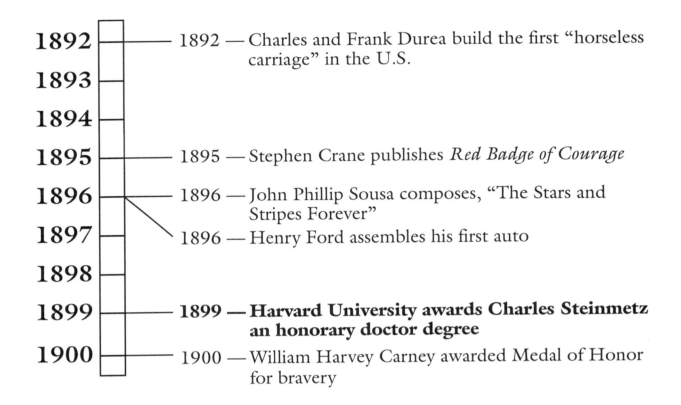

1892 — Charles and Frank Durea build the first "horseless carriage" in the U.S.

1895 — Stephen Crane publishes *Red Badge of Courage*

1896 — John Phillip Sousa composes, "The Stars and Stripes Forever"

1896 — Henry Ford assembles his first auto

1899 — **Harvard University awards Charles Steinmetz an honorary doctor degree**

1900 — William Harvey Carney awarded Medal of Honor for bravery

A WORD ABOUT THE STORY

Charles Steinmetz
MATHEMATICIAN/ENGINEER

The immigration officer who gazed suspiciously at Charles Steinmetz's small twisted body when Steinmetz tried to enter the U.S. might well have taken a moment to remember the old adage, "Don't judge a book by its cover."

The Little Giant

"WELL, I'LL BE —" the gray haired immigration officer nudged the officer next to him. "Look who wants to come to America." The second officer looked up from his desk. Walking towards them was the strangest looking man they had ever seen!

He was a little over four feet—no taller than a nine or ten year old boy—yet he looked like he was in his early twenties. The back of his shoulders stuck out in a strange way, and his face was quite swollen. As he approached, the officers noticed that he walked with a peculiar "hitch"—as if one of his legs were a crutch, and the upper part of his body tilted forward and to the side.

The officers looked at one another. They took their jobs quite seriously. They had to decide whether or not the men, women, and children who had just disembarked from the steamship now docked in the New York harbor were fit enough to stay in America. The American government did not want immigrants who would become burdens to other Americans. America was a growing industrial giant in need of men with strong bodies and working hands, not sickly looking men like —.

The first officer cleared his throat and stared across the desk.

"Namen—your name?" he asked.

"Steinmetz—Carl Steinmetz."

"Do you speak English?"

By now the small man was quite used to the strange stares, but still he was nervous and uncertain. "A few," he muttered. The immigration officer frowned, then gestured to make himself understood as he went on with the questions:

"Do you have a job waiting for you?" Carl shook his head no.

"Do you have any money?" Again Carl shook his head...

FOR A WEEK—as the ship steamed across the Atlantic—Carl and the other poor immigrants had sat or slept cramped closely together, breathing the stale air and eating tasteless food in the lower "steerage" decks. The passengers who had paid full price and had lived and slept on the upper decks had been questioned first. Now—two days later—it was time to question the steerage passengers. They came in search of work and a new life. The year was 1889. America welcomed healthy men able to work—to build bridges, to work in steel mills, to labor in businesses and factories, to drill and shovel tunnels underground, or to dig minerals out of the ground.

The immigration officer reached for his pen. "You have no money, no job, you don't speak English, —." The officer paused "And you do not look very healthy either." He scribbled something on a sheet of paper, then pointed towards a room with a large sign above it. "Go there." he said. Carl turned and stared up at the sign. Printed in ten different languages were the words, DETENTION PEN.

Carl's heart sank. They were going to send him back to Europe! They would not let him in America! He started to say something, to protest in some way, when he heard a familiar voice.

"What is happening here?" It was Oscar Asmussen! Carl's face lit up. Back in Switzerland, Oscar had told him all about America—the land of opportunity, his friend called it. When Oscar said he was leaving for America, Carl decided to go with him.

"This man—he is my friend," Oscar explained. By now he was standing next to Carl. "We came over together."

"We are sending him back," The immigration officer's voice was stern. "He has no job. No money—"

Unlike his small friend, Oscar was neatly dressed and spoke good English. He reached into his pocket and pulled out a roll of bills. "Here, here is money. It is his money. I was holding it for him." It was not exactly the truth, and yet it was, for he certainly would have given it to his friend Carl.

"And he has no job."

Oscar drew in a deep breath. He had been to America before, had lived for a while with his uncle in San Francisco. He explained to the officers that while Carl had no job and while it was easy to see no chance of getting a job that required physical work, he was a bright mathematician—someone who would easily find a job. In fact, he explained, Carl had gone to a university in Germany. "He was a very good student there—he studied mathematics and physics. And chemistry too." It was obvious that Oscar had the attention of the immigration officers now. "He has come to America with me. I will look after him."

The immigration officers took another look at the pathetic looking man in front of them. They still seemed reluctant. Finally, one

America soon discovered that Charles Steinmetz was so much more than a small man who walked in a strange way.

Courtesy, Hall of Electrical History, Schenectady Museum, Schenectady, NY

of them scrawled something on a sheet of paper. "Go," he said.

Oscar and Carl did not wait for more. They grabbed their bags and suitcases and moved towards the sign marked exit. *America at last!*

The immigration officers stared at each other. They said nothing, but it was certain that each was wondering the same thing: Did we make the right decision.

CARL STEINMETZ was born in Germany in 1865. He inherited his unusual stature from his father. When he was 18 he entered a University. He was a bright student, and, after he graduated, he kept attending the university to get his doctor's degree. However, like other college students, Carl spoke out against the German government. One day, a friend told Carl that he had heard that the police were going to arrest Carl. Certain he would be thrown into jail, Carl fled Germany in the middle of the night. He spent the next year in Switzerland where he studied engineering and met Oscar.

CARL ARRIVED IN AMERICA in June of 1889—a time when so much seemed to be happening in the world of invention! Alexander Graham Bell had invented the telephone; Edison was perfecting his electric light; scientists were talking about using electric streetcars. All across America inventors were dreaming up different ways to make use of the wonderful new source of energy called electricity. Scientists knew how to make or "generate" the electricity that was needed for running these inventions. Giant magnets with loops of wire—called generators—were being built alongside America's rivers and waterfalls. *But how do you send this electricity over hundreds of miles without losing the electricity? How do you design electric motors that do not overheat or explode? And how do you make motors that last and that do not waste a lot of electricity?*

Electrical engineers were struggling with these problems about the time Steinmetz came to America. Steinmetz joined a group of engineers who met regularly and listened to their problems. He learned that they wasted a great deal of time trying one design or idea after another—hit or miss—until they found what worked best. Steinmetz showed how they could get the best designs by using mathematical formulas he had worked out. There was no need for "guess work."

The General Electric company soon hired Steinmetz. In two years he was America's greatest electrical engineer. General Electric made him the company's "Chief Consulting Engineer." If anyone ran into a problem while making or designing a new electrical invention, Steinmetz was there to help. In 1899, Harvard University awarded Steinmetz an honorary doctor's degree.

CARL STEINMETZ "FELL IN LOVE" with America. He changed his name to Charles (it sounded more American), learned to speak English, and became a citizen as quickly as he could. In time, he wrote books and magazine articles about electricity to help the ordinary person understand electricity better. Soon newspapers and magazines were writing stories about the scientist they called The Electrical Wizard or The Mastermind or the Tiny Genius or the Little Man With the Giant Mind. Americans soon discovered that Charles Steinmetz was so much more than a small man who walked in a strange way. He was a brilliant mathematician. He enjoyed playing with children, and took an interest in how they were educated. He was generous and cared about the people in his town. America, it seemed, had also fallen in love with the Electrical Wizard.

Charles Steinmetz died in 1923, some thirty four years after an immigration officer had reluctantly agreed to let him stay in America. Newspapers across America ran front page stories about America's beloved "Wizard." The schools in his home town closed for the day. For a full week, the General Electric Company's flag flew at half-mast. As for that immigration officer—he need not have worried. He had, after all, made the right decision.

Writing Activities

1. FIND THE TITLE

Copy out what you think is the best title for this story:

The Little Man With the Great Mind

The Man Who Liked to Joke

Electricity's Early Beginnings

How Electricity Served the People

2. GET THE PICTURE

You are painting some scenes to illustrate the life of Charles Steinmetz. Pick out the THREE scenes that BEST describe him.

Steinmetz copying a mathematical formula

Steinmetz tramping in the forest

Steinmetz working in a laboratory

Steinmetz painting a picture

Steinmetz driving an automobile

Steinmetz taking apart an electric motor

3. IMAGINE

Imagine that someone who knew Charles Steinmetz starts to write about him, but keeps getting interrupted after writing one sentence. Copy ONE of the sentences, and then add two or more of your own.

Steinmetz cared about other people.

Steinmetz made America better.

Steinmetz had many good qualities.

You are Charles Steinmetz. Someone asks you the following questions. How would you answer?

"What advice would you give to someone who has a physical disability?"

"Do you think that America is a land of opportunity?"

Let's Talk—Discussion Activities

4. TAKE A SIDE

Many people have what are sometimes called "handicaps." Some laws have been passed to help so called handicapped people. Take one side or the other, and then give all the reasons you can for the side you take.

We should go out of our way to help a person who has a handicap.

A handicapped person will do better if we do not go out of our way to help.

5. FIND AN ANSWER

What do you think this means: "That person overcame his handicap."

Some people do not like to use the word, "handicapped." Can you explain why?

What do you think the adage, "Don't judge a book by its cover" means? Did you ever "judge a book by its cover," and then turn out to be wrong later? Explain.

We have many electrical conveniences in our homes today thanks to electrical pioneers like Charles Steinmetz and others. If you could only have FIVE of these things that run on electricity, which five would you select? Explain your answers.

lights   vacuum cleaner   television   air conditioner

washing machine   microwave oven   refrigerator   computer

dishwasher   radio

Cooperative Group or Research activities

6. LOOK IT UP

Select one of the persons listed on the time line for this story. Use other books or articles to gather more information about the person, and then make a presentation explaining why the person might be considered a hero.

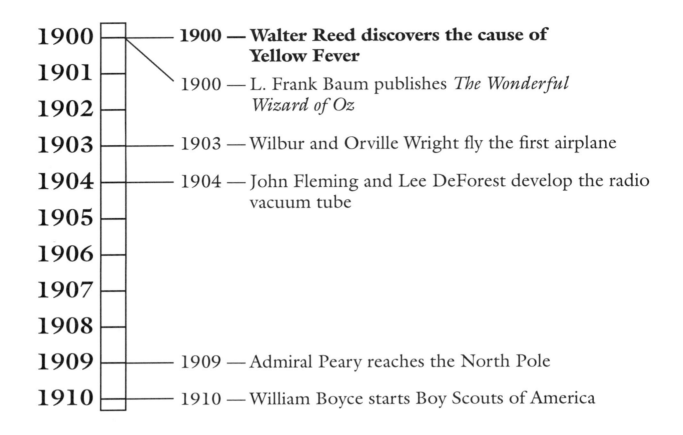

1900	**1900 — Walter Reed discovers the cause of Yellow Fever**
1901	1900 — L. Frank Baum publishes *The Wonderful Wizard of Oz*
1902	
1903	1903 — Wilbur and Orville Wright fly the first airplane
1904	1904 — John Fleming and Lee DeForest develop the radio vacuum tube
1905	
1906	
1907	
1908	
1909	1909 — Admiral Peary reaches the North Pole
1910	1910 — William Boyce starts Boy Scouts of America

A WORD ABOUT THE STORY

Walter Reed
MEDICAL DOCTOR

The mystery had baffled doctors and scientists for centuries: How does the dreaded yellow fever disease spread from one person to another? Army doctor Walter Reed had an idea. If he were right, he could save thousands of lives. But what if he were wrong?

The Experiment

THE THREE MEN looked about the room, then stared at one another, perhaps wondering why they had volunteered. One was a doctor, the other two soldiers. In the center of the room stood a large wooden box. One of the soldiers grabbed a hammer, and began prying away at the top of the box until the heavy wooden lid was loose. Now, together, the three men flipped the top open. A horrible, almost unbearable, smell escaped into the room. The men backed away quickly. They waited a few moments, gathered up their courage, then returned to the box. Muttering as they worked, they pulled the contents out of the box. Out came dirty, filthy blankets, soiled linen, badly stained pillows and pillow cases.

Despite the awful odor, the men some-how managed to place every item on the three army cots in the room. They then sat down to rest. Along one wall of the 14 by 20 foot room, a stove blasted out a steady stream of hot air. Next to the stove stood tubs filled with water to insure that the men would breathe only moist or humid air. The single tightly screened door to the outside was locked, and behind it was yet another door. There were two windows next to the door—both of them locked and well screened.

Later that night, the soldiers tossed and turned in their cots. As they tried their best to get comfortable, they thought about what the doctors had told them earlier: *it will not be a pleasant stay... you will live this way for about three weeks... you will get paid a few hundred dollars*. But probably what stuck most in their minds as they drifted off to sleep was the doctors' final word of warning—*and you may not come out of this alive.*

These men were trying to help doctors solve a strange mystery—a mystery that had baffled the world for centuries...

SOME FIVE MONTHS BEFORE, on a June afternoon in 1900, a ship docked at the steamy Havana harbor in Cuba, and four solemn faced men—all doctors—walked down the gangplank. They had good reason to look as concerned as they did. The lives of thousands of people lay in their hands. Dr. Walter Reed was in charge. The son of a minister, Reed had decided very early in his life that he wanted to be a doctor and help others. He had spent the past 25 years serving as a physician in the U.S. Army and had risen to the rank of major. In 1898, the U.S. went to war with Spain. U.S. soldiers invaded the Spanish owned island of Cuba. The once mighty Spanish empire no longer had the army or the navy to carry on much of a war, and so, a few months after the war began, Spain surrendered. The United States took over many of Spain's island possessions, in-cluding the large island of Cuba, nestled in the Caribbean some 90 miles off the coast of Florida.

While Americans at home were celebrat-ing the victory, officials in the American government grew very concerned about reports coming back from Cuba. A horrible disease called "yellow fever," was killing more American soldiers than all the guns fired during the war. Cubans were also dying from the disease. Major Walter Reed was given the order: *Go to Cuba, and stop this terrible scourge.*

SOON AFTER THEY ARRIVED, the four doctors made their rounds of the Army hospital. They saw the patients, and spoke to their doctors and nurses. A picture soon emerged of the horrors of a yellow fever attack. First there were chills and a headache. The patient's back and arms and legs began to ache—badly. Then came an awful high fever. The fever could last a few hours, or rage on for days. In the meantime, the patient began to turn a tell-tale yellow—a certain sign the liver was affected and that the patient had yellow fever. Finally, the fever and the pains stopped! The patient began to feel better. The disease, however, was only playing a cruel trick: sometimes the patient recovered, but many times the fever came back worse than ever. Some people survived; many did not.

SHAKEN BY WHAT THEY SAW and heard, Major Walter Reed and the other doctors grew all the more determined to do something. *But what?* The disease had raged for centuries. No doctor, no scientists had ever been able to stop its spread. What made Walter Reed think that he could solve the Yellow Fever mystery?

Once the disease hit a village, town, or city, there seemed to be no clue, no hint, as to just who would get the disease. It might attack one person in a home, skip others in the family as well as neighbors on either side, and then strike again two or three doors down. It seemed vicious and cunning—and unbeatable. People steered clear of anyone who had the disease or who lived in the same

home with a victim. Doctors, hoping to stop the disease from spreading, told families to bury or burn all of a victim's possessions—his clothes, furniture, bedding. But one thing was certain—doctors did not really know how the disease spread; they were only guessing.

Walter Reed decided to do more than guess. He wanted to test whether or not coming in contact with a victim's possessions or bedding really spread yellow fever. The experiments began on a November day in 1900 with one of the doctors and two soldiers—all volunteers—placed in a hot, humid, tightly screened room. A nervous group of doctors waited out each day. Some three weeks later, they had their results: *Not a single volunteer had yellow fever.* The experiment was repeated a second, and then a third time with other volunteers. Victims' clothing and even more foul smelling bedding was brought in. The result: not a single case of yellow fever. Dr. Reed had proved that the clothing and bedding of a victim did not spread the disease.

Then what did?

YEARS BEFORE, a doctor, noticing how the disease jumped from place to place, claimed that insects somehow carried the disease. Other scientists laughed at this idea, but Reed only wondered. Meantime, a Cuban doctor named Carlos Finlay had spent a good deal of time researching the disease. He believed that a certain type of mosquito was the cause of the disease. Most doctors ignored the idea. Dr. Reed did not. He met with Dr. Finlay and listened attentively to what he had to say. Dr. Reed then made a decision: he would begin experiments to find out if, indeed, mosquitoes could spread the disease. There was a problem with doing any experimenting however. As far as the doctors knew at that time, there was only one living thing that caught the disease—a human being.

A LARGE ROOM was built with beds on either side. A fine tight screen ran down its center from floor to ceiling, splitting the room exactly in half. Seven volunteers entered one half of the room. Another volunteer entered the other side of the room. There were no boxes of dirty bedding to empty. Clean, white sheets, neatly folded blankets, and spotless pillows covered the cots on both sides. No stoves spewed out heat, and there were no tubs of water to raise the air's humidity. The first group had only to sit and wait. The man on the other side, separated only by the screen, was promised that special "guests" would be arriving shortly.

The "guests" arrived soon enough. They were fifteen mosquitoes that had bitten yellow fever victims at a certain stage of the disease. The mosquitoes found their way to the volunteer's bare arms, and bit him a number of times. The screen, however, kept them away from the others in the room.

The single volunteer soon came down with a bad case of Yellow Fever, but much to the joy of the doctors, did recover from his illness. On the other hand, *none* of the men on the other side of the room caught yellow fever. Still more experiments were done, and then Dr. Walter Reed announced he had the answer to the question that had puzzled the

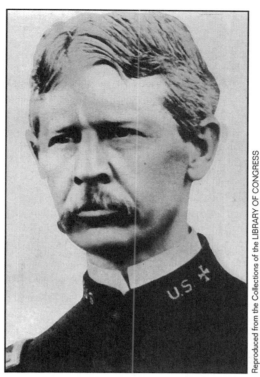

Reproduced from the Collections of the LIBRARY OF CONGRESS

Major Reed was given the order: Stop this terrible scourge

world: *Yellow fever was spread by a certain type of mosquito.*

The question remained: How do you get rid of the mosquitoes? Using fly swatters and nets was no real solution. The answer: If you go after the mosquito's eggs, the mosquitoes would be gone in a short time. But how do you do that? The solution was brilliant, but simple. The doctors knew mosquitoes laid their eggs in still water—on ponds, in lakes, atop tubs or pots left outside. *Why not spray the still water everywhere with a fine spray of oil?* And this is just what was done. The oil floated on top of the water keeping the eggs from ever turning into mosquitoes.

IN 1900 THERE WERE THOUSANDS of cases of yellow fever in Cuba. A few years later, there were none! Yellow fever had come to the Americas and the islands of the Caribbean in the early in the 1600's. Over the next three centuries, the stories were always the same. An epidemic would start up, and spread through a town or city. Thousands of people would desert the town or city and flee in terror. In the U.S., most of the epidemics struck in the hot, humid summer months in Southern towns. Similar stories were told in other warm parts of the world. But now, the word was out—thanks to the work of Major Walter Reed and the doctors who worked with him, the scourge that had plagued the world for centuries had been conquered.

1900

Written Activities

1. FIND THE TITLE

Copy out what you think is the best title for this story:

The Major Who Came to Cuba

The Doctor Who Conquered Yellow Fever

The Cuban Story

The End of the Spanish American War

2. GET THE PICTURE

You are painting some scenes to illustrate the life of Walter Reed. Pick out the THREE scenes that BEST describe him.

He is —

— riding in a car   — looking at a test tube

— visiting a hospital   — checking his rifle

— laughing and joking — staring at a mosquito

3. IMAGINE

A time machine brings you back to meet Walter Reed. What three questions would you ask him?

Imagine you are Walter Reed. Describe how you felt when you discovered what caused yellow Fever.

Imagine that you are describing Walter Reed to a friend. Pick out the FOUR words that you would most likely use.

muddled   wise   confused   intelligent

persistent   cruel   determined   ordinary